What people are saying about …

CHASING SUPERWOMAN

"Finally a voice that modern day moms can relate to. *Chasing Superwoman* gives today's working mothers the laughter and encouragement they so desperately need as they struggle to balance faith, family, and friendships from the front lines of working America."

Michelle LaRowe, executive director of the International Nanny Association, mom, and author of *Working Mom's 411, A Mom's Ultimate Book of Lists*, and *Nanny to the Rescue!*

"*Chasing Superwoman* is a beautifully simple story of the faith journey of a working mother learning to balance work, family, and marriage while trying to define her own calling to be a disciple of Christ. Susan DiMickele offers not only practical advice but also encouragement to women who struggle to be all things to all people—all the time. DiMickele tells her story with humor, grace, and a sense of humility, describing the challenges of discipleship for all people of faith in a world where God is increasingly marginalized and roles are not always clearly defined. Women will identify with her narrative and appreciate her realization that by the grace of God, we are all freed from the need to be perfect. A highly recommended read for working mothers—and fathers."

Bishop Callon Holloway, Southern Ohio Synod of the Evangelical Lutheran Church Association

CHASING SUPERWOMAN

CHASING SUPERWOMAN

A WORKING MOM'S ADVENTURES IN LIFE AND FAITH

SUSAN M. DiMICKELE

CHASING SUPERWOMAN
Published by David C. Cook
4050 Lee Vance View
Colorado Springs, CO 80918 U.S.A.

David C. Cook Distribution Canada
55 Woodslee Avenue, Paris, Ontario, Canada N3L 3E5

David C. Cook U.K., Kingsway Communications
Eastbourne, East Sussex BN23 6NT, England

David C. Cook and the graphic circle C logo
are registered trademarks of Cook Communications Ministries.

Some names have been changed for privacy purposes.

LCCN 2010924060
ISBN 978-1-4347-6462-1
eISBN 978-0-7814-0450-1

Published in association with the literary agency of WordServe Literary Group, Ltd., 10152 S. Knoll Circle, Highlands Ranch, CO 80130.

The Team: Susan Tjaden, Amy Kiechlin, Sarah Schultz, Caitlyn York, Karen Athen

Cover design and illustration: The DesignWorks Group, Connie Gabbert

Printed in the United States of America
First Edition 2010

1 2 3 4 5 6 7 8 9 10

031910

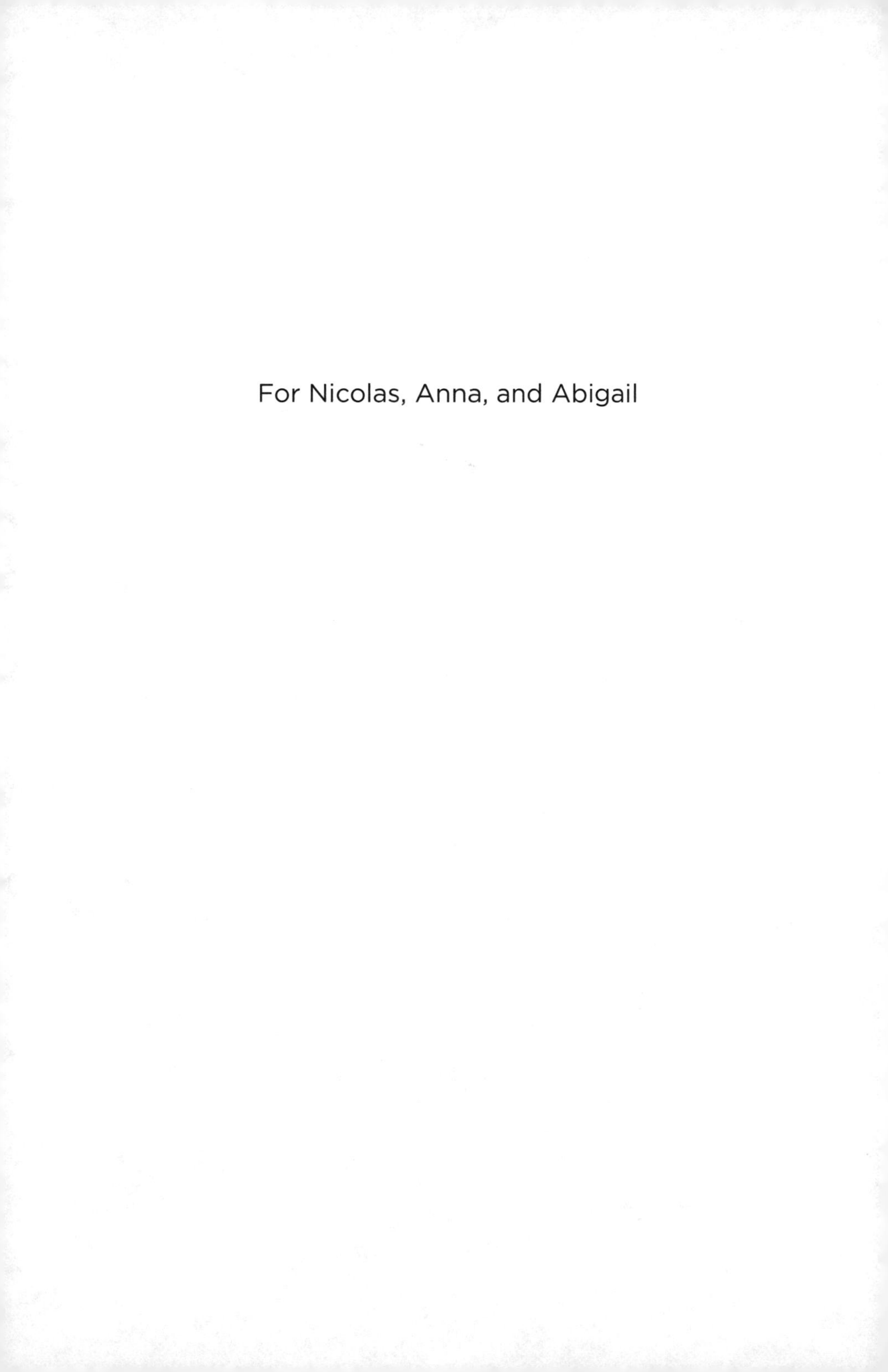

For Nicolas, Anna, and Abigail

Contents

Acknowledgments

I love the story of Jesus healing the ten blind men. Unfortunately, I identify more with the nine who rode off into the sunset instead of the one man who came back to say thanks. Because I'm one of those people who always forget to send thank-you notes, I'm going to say thank you here, right up front.

Truth is, I could never attempt to be Superwoman—let alone write about it—without all the wonderful family and friends surrounding me, starting with my parents. Thanks, Mom and Dad, for your love, faith, simplicity, and devotion to family and each other. I'm so proud to be your daughter. And my four wonderful sisters—Mona, MaryBeth, Amy, and Janie—you are my best friends for life. As the saying goes, "a sister is a friend forever."

Of course so many others inspire and support me on a daily basis, like the Go Fish Women; Jane Armstrong; Bishop Holloway; Pastor Eric and my friends at Upper Arlington Lutheran Church; my colleagues at the firm; my neighbors on Henthorn Road; my prayer partner, Cheryl; and my Bible study partners, Shelly and Jen, who hang out with me late at night, keep me laughing, and help me to see beyond myself.

I knew absolutely nothing about the publishing process until I connected with my fabulous agent, Rachelle Gardner. Thanks, Rachelle, for taking on a first-time author and opening the door to the team at David C. Cook. And a very special thanks to my editor and now dear friend, Susan Tjaden. Last, but certainly not least, thank you to my husband, Doug, for always putting our family first and for supporting me as I spent many evenings in front of my laptop while you wondered what the heck I was up to! Now you finally know.

Introduction

Can a mother of young children be at the top of her profession without sacrificing her family or her faith? Will society and the Christian community allow her to try?

As a mother of three young children in a fast-paced legal career, I wrestled deeply with these questions. What had other mothers written to address this dilemma? While I found lots of good books on parenting and managing life as a working mother—like finding a good day care, better managing my time, or putting the family on some unrealistic carpool schedule—I was surprised that no one had written candidly about the complex spiritual struggles of the working mother. Lots of people out there had advice, but I was more interested in an authentic dialogue. I knew from talking with my friends that so many of us have the same questions, and we're really tired of it when someone gives us the same old pat answers we have heard over and over again. Even more troubling, none of the working-mother books I could find even addressed a working woman of faith. It was as if faith was completely divorced from the lives of all working mothers.

Hence the idea for *Chasing Superwoman* was born. Of course I had a lot of excuses as to why it wasn't the right time to write a book. Between practicing law full time, maintaining a healthy marriage, taking care of three young children, and family and friends who needed my attention in between, I could never find the time to write a book. Besides, I couldn't even find time for *me,* not to mention a relationship with God, so I figured I'd probably have to wait until retirement to write this. Life was full for the next decade or two.

I might have just stopped there, but I'm incredibly impatient. I couldn't quit thinking, "If not me, then who?" While the Christian community sometimes operates under the assumption that the only women attending church are traditional stay-at-home moms who act like the Church Lady and belong to the PTA, this stereotype doesn't address the fact that more than 75 percent of mothers with school-aged children work outside the home.[1] As one of these women, I needed to write a book that would address our faith *and* our lifestyle.

Most parents agree that one of our greatest challenges is the spiritual development of our children. As parents, we must have an authentic and vibrant faith to provide meaningful spiritual guidance to our children.[2] Yet mothers like me who work outside the home arguably have less control over our children—making it even more challenging for us to model a vibrant faith and ensure that our children receive our much-needed attention. In writing *Chasing Superwoman,* I confront the basic fears and insecurities of most working mothers through my own imperfect and humbling experiences—will my children turn out okay? How can I make sure I tend to their spiritual development? And can I really trust God to take care of them, even when I'm not there?

I know other working mothers must wonder, *Am I the only one who feels like a bad mommy when my cell phone won't stop ringing in the pediatrician's office?* Most of us are running ourselves ragged, pretending to be Superwoman, and feeling guilty when we achieve something less than superhero perfection. Who says we can't have it all? The problem? It's a miserable existence to run around in circles and try to do it all yourself. Most days, I fall far short of being Superwoman—I'm tired of chasing perfection, and I just really want someone to carry me. (Okay, I'd even settle for a day at the spa.) The other problem? I don't want anyone to put me in a box—especially when I've yet to figure it out myself. So, if I've learned anything through my adventures as a working mother it's this: Only by God's grace do each of us have the freedom to run her own course, and a loving and gracious God will be paving the way—even holding us at times—every step of the journey.

I'm blessed to have a supportive husband who stands beside me as I wrestle with it all. When I told Doug I was going to write a book about the struggles of being a working mother, he was instantly supportive. But he also said he had one rule. He gave me his serious, piercing look so I couldn't later claim I thought he was joking and said, "You're not allowed to write about me."

So I really tried hard to respect his privacy, and I went out of my way to completely avoid mentioning him in my first writings. I didn't write about our first date to the homecoming dance or the fact that we were high school sweethearts or that he put me through law school on a shoestring budget. And I didn't dare write about the ups and downs of marriage, our disagreements over parenting, his distrust of organized religion, or his arm's-length relationship with the church. I left out the part about how he stayed home with the kids full time after our caregiver's adoption and until Abby could enter preschool—even though it cost Doug his own career and temporary sanity. I really *wanted* to write about the incredible romance that still exists after sixteen years of marriage and the thick glue that holds us together tighter than ever, but I knew he would die of embarrassment and would probably kill me if I put all the details on paper. So I simply left him out.

As hard as I tried to keep him out of the first draft of my manuscript, I could tell something was missing. *He* was missing. So I said to him, "You know, I really can't write a book about my life unless you're in it."

It was hard for him to argue with my point.

Doug suggested a compromise: "Just don't use my real name."

So I tried writing about being married and raising kids with Rob, but it just wasn't the same. All my neighbors and friends would read it and think I was getting divorced, or worse, was some kind of polygamist. So I went back to calling him Doug. I just warned him that if he wanted any editorial control over the book he would have to get involved in my writing.

He graciously left me to my own devices.

I'm also thankful to have three amazing children to write about. At the time I wrote this book, they were ages seven, four, and two. Nick is my firstborn who thinks deeply about life and follows the rules. He is followed by Anna who is my princess and fashion queen. Abby is our baby—we can't imagine life without her because she makes us laugh and keeps us young. Like most working mothers, I wear lots of superhero capes, but my mommy cape is by far my favorite.

As a lawyer, I fully admit that I'm writing from a narrow perspective, and some of my nonlawyer friends tell me it's hard to relate to the world of Lady Lawyer. I apologize for that up front. It's all I know. Lady Lawyer has a nasty habit of talking down to just about everyone when she's in her element, and I'm thankful that I have Doug to regularly remind me when I get too far off on my high horse. I don't pretend to understand or even typify most working mothers, many of whom have jobs that would make Lady Lawyer feel silly for complaining even the slightest bit about her own demands and struggles. I only hope that my journey can resonate with the millions of hard-working mothers out there who, for a variety of reasons, spend much of their days away from their young children and pray in their hearts that everything will turn out okay in the end.

While I write from a decidedly Christian perspective, I hope that my writing will be inspiring to all working mothers who struggle on their own faith journeys. Yes, the road can be a steep climb, but I wouldn't trade it for anything. Thanks in advance for sharing this journey with me. Together, I pray that we can stop chasing Superwoman.

ONE

The Superwoman Within

> In a word, what I'm saying is, Grow up. You're kingdom subjects. Now live like it. Live out your God-created identity. Live generously and graciously toward others, the way God lives toward you.
>
> Matthew 5:48 (MSG)

Most people hate lawyers. This is why so many lawyers marry other lawyers—no one else likes them. Fortunately, I met my husband, Doug, before I became a lawyer, and he still likes me. At least that's what he tells me.

If I have to be honest, I really don't like Lady Lawyer. She brings out the worst in me. Given the choice, I would much rather put on my mommy cape and play Devoted Mommy. But most days and more nights and weekends than I would care to admit, Devoted Mommy is busy playing Lady Lawyer. I didn't set out to give Lady Lawyer this much power. It just sort of happened. I always insisted my career would take a backseat to the more important things in life—my family, my faith, my soul. I never thought Lady Lawyer would move in, take over, fire the staff, and change my identity. She's known to get her way. Lady Lawyer is shrewd, self-sufficient, demanding, impatient, and arrogant. She gets right to the point and doesn't waste your time. Why would any of her clients pay her exorbitant hourly rate in six-minute increments for anything less than the best? She doesn't make mistakes, and if you work for Lady Lawyer you'd better not make any mistakes either. The standard is perfection. Who said anything about forgiveness? There are no second chances.

Devoted Mommy is quite the opposite. She's warm and patient. She wastes lots of time picking up toys, reading books, and sitting on the floor playing patty-cake. As much as she likes to be efficient, her children always want to help her, so everything takes twice as long, and she makes lots of mistakes and lots of messes. Devoted Mommy knows the important thing is to say you are sorry and ask and receive forgiveness. After all, no one is perfect.

Okay, maybe Devoted Mommy isn't warm and patient *all* the time and maybe she would turn into Evil Mommy part of the time if she stayed at home with her kids all day, but you get the point. Lady Lawyer would make a terrible mother, which is why I have to keep her away from the children. Not to mention she has a terrible mouth on her. It's not intentional. It's just that most lawyers don't understand plain English unless it is laced with heavy profanity.

If only I could play Devoted Mommy more often.

The Evils of Television

At least Lady Lawyer and Devoted Mommy actually have something in common. They both hate television. Lady Lawyer has better things to do. For her, TV is the ultimate waste of time and an exercise in inefficiency. Simply put, TV is for idiots. It's mind-numbing, unenlightening, and unproductive. Why watch TV when you can bill hours instead? So Lady Lawyer watches TV only as a last resort, when she's multitasking. Sometimes it's faster to catch the local news and major world events on the tube. It becomes a necessary evil.

Devoted Mommy hates TV for different reasons. It's not a necessary evil, it's just plain evil. It's like inviting the Devil into your home and asking him to raise your children. "Gee, Satan, would you do me a favor and watch the kids for a few hours, 'cause I'm really busy right now and I'd prefer to have them hypnotized and brain-dead so that I can get some work done."

The other day while I was playing Weekend Mommy, Doug and seven-year-old Nick were watching *The Bad News Bears*. I was appalled. The language was filthy. These snotty-nosed kids and their recalcitrant coach had no respect for authority or each other, and Nick would soon be talking like a potty mouth if we continued to let this trash into our living room. Suddenly, Devoted Mommy transformed into Fundamentalist Mommy.

"I don't want to hear that language in our house ever again, and I want that filthy show turned off." Doug and Nick just looked at me. I continued, "TV is straight from the pit of hell and I can't sit by and watch you fill your brain with this garbage."

Doug may be incorrigible, but I still have to exercise some moral authority over my children.

I learned that from my own mother. We had knock-down, drag-out fights over *Three's Company* and *Charlie's Angels*. I would sneak downstairs and watch these shows with my older sisters over my mother's deep disapproval. (Which was worse, Jack and Chrissy living in sin, or Farrah Fawcett showing her cleavage? I never got an answer, I just knew they were both bad.) What kind of mother would I be if I let *The Bad News Bears* ruin Nick's innocence and lead him down a path of destruction?

So later that night, after I put the girls to bed, I told Nick that we needed to talk. We sat in his bed before prayers, as we do every night, and I explained to him that some things on TV are wrong, and the Bad News Bears really shouldn't say bad words.

"Did you hear bad words in the movie today?"

Nick responded, "I'm not sure. I know *stupid* is a bad word." Nick is a smart kid, so he saw this as an opportunity to ask me, point-blank, what the other bad words were that had caused me so much concern. Now I was stuck. Fundamentalist Mommy was going to have to feed her own son swear words. So we talked about how "hell" is a bad word, and why you wouldn't want to tell someone to "go to hell," because that's where Satan lives.

Nick asked, "Is it still okay to say 'for heaven's sake'?"

"Yes," I said. "That's still okay."

I was thankful he still had some innocence left. And I didn't have the heart to tell him the other bad words in the show. We'll save that for another day. Fundamentalist Mommy can take a rest for now.

Sunday School

I don't turn into Fundamentalist Mommy very often. But Devoted Mommy clearly needed to have more of a spiritual focus, especially with Lady Lawyer sucking her dry all those hours during the week. I actually prefer the term "Spiritual Mommy." The Fundamentalist label has way too much baggage, even though I'm thankful for my roots.

So Spiritual Mommy decided to teach Sunday school. I could kill two birds with one stone and spend quality time with the kids on the weekend while exerting Spiritual Mommy's much-needed moral authority. Maybe I could even reverse some of the brain injury from all that TV.

Given my schedule during the week, Doug and most of my friends thought I was downright crazy for taking on another weekend responsibility. "Suz, just what you need, another thing to add to your schedule. Haven't you ever heard of the word *no?*"

Actually, since I became a mother, *no* has almost evaporated from my vocabulary. I reserve it for when I really need it—like when I'm asked to make cupcakes for the bake sale, organize the parent phone tree, or volunteer to be the lunch monitor during lunch bunch. After all, I can't do *everything,* right? But when it comes to the spiritual development of my children, Devoted Mommy reminds me that, unlike baking cookies or being a lunch monitor, I really can't delegate that one very easily.

To my pleasant surprise, Sunday school became my favorite hour of the week. I wear casual clothes and comfortable shoes, sing silly songs, play duck-duck-goose, and sit on the floor with the children while teaching them that God is your friend, even when you can't see Him.

I remember my own Sunday school days vividly like they were yesterday. I'll never forget that poster in my classroom of Jesus knocking on the door to your heart. Of course there's no door handle because the door can be opened only from the inside. It was during that Sunday school class that I asked Jesus to come into my heart. Some people say that young children can't understand spiritual things, but I beg to differ. Life has become much too complicated. Sometimes I want to go back to the simple faith of my childhood, but I can't. So I do the next best thing. I live vicariously through my children. I never realized until after I became a parent how entirely normal it is to live vicariously through your children. Every parent does it. That's why so many of us spend inordinate amounts of money on Christmas gifts and Disney World. (Who said anything about the kids?) I barely remember going to Disney World with my parents, although they love to talk about it like it was yesterday. I hear the same stories over and over again: "Remember when Susan screamed and cried because she wanted to go on the rides with her older sisters, and then we had to ride 'It's a Small World' over and over again?"

I used to think, "Don't they get tired of telling these old stories? Do they really think anyone is listening?"

Now I understand why.

Lady Lawyer, of course, doesn't have time during the week to prepare for Sunday school. It would cut into her billable hours. Yet sometimes Spiritual Mommy convinces her to help gather Sunday school materials, particularly if it involves Internet shopping. I looked all over the Internet for that picture of Christ knocking and finally found one that is similar to my own childhood memories. I ordered it immediately—the shipping and handling cost more than the poster, but I willingly gave over my credit card number. It was worth every penny.

The Unveiling of the *Mona Lisa*

When the Jesus picture arrived, Nick and Anna were bursting with curiosity. How many of my online purchases arrive in a long tube the size of Texas? Lady Lawyer had outdone herself. *A new toy? A treasure map?* The possibilities were endless. Unfortunately, the kids always raid the mail before I get home from work. I should have had the picture sent to my office, like I do with Christmas gifts. Last Christmas I bought Doug a new office chair online and sent it straight to my office. The only problem I hadn't considered was getting it home. The box was too heavy for me to carry from my office tower to the parking garage, so I had to beg a few guys in my office to help. That cost Lady Lawyer a few favors. But a poster? I could have carried that myself.

Nick and Anna desperately wanted to open it, but I told them they would have to wait for Sunday school. It was going to be like the unveiling of the *Mona Lisa*. I could hardly wait myself. At minimum, I needed a sneak preview. After all, what if they had sent the wrong picture? It might be a poster of Daniel in the lion's den, the last temptation of Christ, or worse yet, what if they had mistakenly sent some trash from a pornographic site? I couldn't take that risk with the spiritual future of fifteen preschoolers resting on my shoulders. So after the kids went to bed, I pulled out the poster. I gazed at the picture longingly, relieved to see Jesus knocking in the familiar scene. For the next fifteen minutes, I couldn't stop staring. Could faith be this simple? Maybe when I was five years old, but not now. Not in my world.

For most people, seeing is believing. "Show me the money." "Do you have the goods?" "The proof is in the pudding." I get tired of living by these rules all week. Preschoolers are different. Their hearts have not yet been hardened by the cold reality of the real world. Most of them haven't been sued yet.

Maybe if I just brought the picture of Christ knocking and put it in my office, in place of my diploma, things at work would be more spiritual. I know that Jesus is there, even when I can't see Him, but I frankly forget about Him when I step into my office. Spiritual Mommy thought it was an excellent idea to bring the poster to work. That way, when Lady Lawyer gets out of line, she can just look at Jesus knocking and be reminded of her deep faith. I've been told my office really needs to be redecorated.

Lady Lawyer quickly squashed that idea. People would think I had completely cracked. Besides, lots of people would be offended. What would happen if the six o'clock news came to get a headshot of me at my desk and the picture of Christ knocking was hanging in the background? The audience would think my law firm was some kind of religious cult, and I'd never hear the end of it.

So I left the picture of Christ knocking at home. One of these days when Lady Lawyer is shopping on the Net, I'm going to make her order a frame. We'll hang the framed picture right next to the TV. That way, when Doug and Nick are watching *The Bad News Bears* or some other trashy show and I'm not there to turn it off, Jesus will gently remind them that TV is evil.

Better yet, we'll hang it in place of the TV.

One of the Sunday school parents asked me if I was a teacher. I laughed out loud. When I told her I was a lawyer, she looked surprised. Spiritual Mommy had successfully kept Lady Lawyer muzzled, which isn't easy to do. I took her surprise as a compliment, and said thank you. I explained to her that the reason I enjoy teaching Sunday school so much is that it is so dramatically different from my everyday life. After dealing all week with grown-up problems, complex legal issues, and the politics of a large law firm, I welcome Silly Putty and puppet shows.

I've gotten good at checking my lawyer cape at the door when it comes to church. No suit, no high heels, not too much lipstick, no cell phone or BlackBerry, no dirty looks, no potty mouth, and lots of confession and forgiveness. I wear my hair down with comfortable shoes and suburban clothes, smiling pleasantly while I'm holding Abby in one arm and my Sunday school bag in the other. Let's face it—most parents don't have high expectations of a Sunday school teacher. They just want an hour of peace.

But teaching Sunday school has its low points too. Even Devoted Mommy gets tired of cutting out crafts late on Saturday nights and waking up early on Sunday mornings to get three kids out the door. Sometimes I wake up on Sunday morning and I'm sick and I can't find a substitute, or my kids are sick and I want to stay home and take care of them, but I can't. Sometimes my class is rambunctious, and I don't have a helper and they all have to go to the bathroom at the same time, or one of the kids freaks out, or I just feel like being with my own kids instead of spreading myself so thin. Sometimes I think it's not fair to leave Abby in the nursery for another hour and I miss her and wish she could join us in Sunday school, but the few times I have brought her I have been completely unable to give the rest of the class any attention.

Sometimes the whole class is staring into space and I don't think anyone is listening to the lesson, but I still know I am planting seeds.

My Sunday school class is filled with your typical upper-middle-class children, and while most of them are from loving homes, some of them are beginning to struggle with things that no one can adequately explain. Terminal illness of a loved one. Divorce. Even death. One little boy in my class, we'll call him Charlie, lost his daddy last year. When I pulled out the picture of Jesus knocking, Charlie's eyes locked mine, and I knew that he needed to know that Jesus would always be there and would never leave him, so I looked into Charlie's eyes and said, "Once Jesus comes into your heart, He will never leave."

The next week, Charlie's grandma stopped me after class and told me that Charlie had asked Jesus to come into his heart. I gave her a big hug and we both fought back the tears. Charlie doesn't come to class as much as he used to, and I know it's hard for his grandma to bring him on the weekends, but I still had the privilege of planting a few seeds.

I like planting seeds. It beats billable hours. Lady Lawyer can't say, "Sorry I didn't get the agreement done, but I planted a few seeds." Or, "I know we lost the case, but I laid some groundwork for next time. Give it a few years and you'll see some results." Her clients would fire her.

Sunday school teachers don't have to worry about getting fired. Why? Because we teach Sunday school for free. It's not like there's a long line of volunteers waiting to take over. If you pass the criminal background and reference check and like kids, you're in.

The second we start paying Sunday school teachers, I'm done. Who wants the pressure of another billable hour? Not me. Some things money can't buy. Besides, even Lady Lawyer needs to hang up her cape on the weekends.

Can Superwoman really live in two worlds? What is really behind the cape, and am I ever going to figure out my true identity? And what does it mean to live out my "God-created identity"?[1] I know there aren't easy answers, but that still doesn't stop me from asking the questions. Sometimes I wonder, *Who am I really chasing anyway?*

TWO

Superwoman Has a Day Job

Whatever you do, work at it with all your heart, as working for the Lord, not for men.

Colossians 3:23

Nick always asks me why I work while other moms stay home. There's no simple answer. The easy answer is that I work for money. But that's not the only reason I work. This isn't the answer I gave him.

What working mother hasn't had her children ask her why she works? It's a fair question with a host of possible answers. Money, of course, is the easiest concept for kids to understand. Some of my friends tell their children, "Mommy works so that we can pay for our house," or, "If I don't go to work today, we might not be able to go on vacation this year." While I often resort to these easy answers, I also try to explain to Nick that God gives us all gifts and talents, and I'm simply trying to do my best at my job. I go on to explain that, while I would rather not go to work some days, I believe it is the right thing to do, even though it can be hard. Nick understands that it's important to do your best, but he also understands that a job provides money, which isn't a bad lesson in and of itself, but I never want him to think that work is only about money. Work is about so much more.

Some working mothers set out to pursue a career with determination and never even consider staying at home full time to raise children. Others don't have a road map or master plan, and while we constantly feel the tug between home and work, most days we are thankful for our jobs. Still other working mothers would rather not work at all, but we simply need the income to provide for our families. I'm a mix. While I can't imagine life without my lawyer cape, sometimes the life of Lady Lawyer is a handful to juggle with small children.

Sometimes I envy my friends who work out of their homes, like Self-Employed Stefanie, my best friend from college. Stefanie and I never missed a party or a social gathering in college, and unlike me she wanted nothing more than to start a family in her twenties and be a full-time mom. But life doesn't always turn out as planned. When her husband was without an income and they had a young child to support, she started a part-time home business that became successful (she's more driven than she likes to admit), and now she and her husband work together, out of their home, in a family business. So in between client calls she bakes casseroles, and she takes breaks during the day for carpool duty—but that just means her workday lasts longer and starts earlier than most.

There's no easy path for a working mother. In fact, Self-Employed Stefanie will tell you that working out of your home with small children can make life more complicated, not less. At least Lady Lawyer gets to sit at her desk and drink coffee without the distractions of screaming children and dirty laundry. So even though I spend more hours away from home than Self-Employed Stefanie, neither of us can claim the other has an easier day.

My best friend from law school, Sassy Shelly, also works out of her home to be with her four kids, three dogs, and five cats. I don't know how she gets any work done, but she never studied in law school and always seemed to get by just fine. Unlike most of my classmates, she wasn't uptight or intimidated. While everyone else was fighting over the library carrels and the study guides, Sassy Shelly and I shunned the library and regularly met at the coffee shop to study. Instead of studying, however, we always ended up debating religion or politics. Sassy Shelly would always take the opposite position of mine, and she would argue that religion was for the illiterate masses, uneducated, and weak. The great thing about Sassy Shelly is she has an opinion about everything, and she knows something about everything, which makes her one of the best conversationalists on the planet. Studying could wait. World problems needed to first be solved, and I cherished those times together, even if we never got any studying done.

Now that Shelly is married with four young children, we don't hang out in coffee shops and debate politics nearly enough. She's one tough lawyer, and like me, she's trying to juggle it all. So when I call her from work and hear her kids and the dogs in the background, I'm reminded that the peace and quiet of my office isn't so bad after all. She and Self-Employed Stefanie remind me to be careful what I wish for when I complain about spending too much time at the office.

Sassy Shelly and I always complain that we don't have jobs that actually help people. Why didn't we become nurses who save lives, or teachers who impact the lives of sweet little children? Instead, Shelly is busy helping her company ship more jobs overseas, and I'm busy working at one of the largest and most prestigious law firms in the world. We represent business. Big business. Sometimes I wonder how that fits into my faith or into motherhood.

My Lawyer Cape

When I started practicing law, my other college roommate, Built Becky—an Olympic cyclist who looks more like a body builder—framed a verse for me that I still hang in my office: "Whatever you do, work at it with all your heart, as working for the Lord, not for men."[1] I'll confess, I haven't looked at that verse in a while, and I hardly see myself working for God these days. What, if anything, about my workday is spiritual? Can I seriously claim that I'm working for the Lord? My clients call me when they get sued, get in legal trouble, or want to fire someone. No one calls me up to say, "Hey, I was hoping you could help me do some work for God today."

Instead, Lady Lawyer has become an expert at firing people. I wonder sometimes, did Jesus ever fire anyone? If so, He certainly didn't make money off of the deal. I also can't find any evidence that He billed by the hour.

Lady Lawyer also has to skip the Bible passages that say "blessed are the peacemakers." She's always in the middle of a fight. The better advocate I am, the better result for my client. If clients wanted to throw the towel in and make peace, they wouldn't hire me in the first place. And if you think I'm tough you should see Sassy Shelly or Jock Jill in action. Jock Jill—my best friend at the firm and one of the toughest lawyers you will ever meet—can take down a room of lawyers with one swing, and Sassy Shelly can outwit (and outtalk) even the best of the best with her silver tongue. It's nothing personal. Just business.

I was having lunch with my friend Bleeding-Heart Brian and our pastor, Eric. Bleeding-Heart Brian is another friend from law school (he was in the group that was in the library carrels while Sassy Shelly and I were at the coffee shop), and he was trying to explain the daily battles and utter spiritual void in the practice of law.

"You enter a battle every day. It's like jumping from an airplane into enemy territory without backup. You have to have all of your gear, and you can't let your guard down for a second. You are trying to be as much of a jerk as you can, because your client expects it and you are trying to get the best deal possible for your client. The attorney on the other side is trying to do the exact same thing. It's all-out war. There's no room to turn the other cheek or play nice guy. The biggest jerk usually wins."

It's hard for me to refute Bleeding-Heart Brian's rendition of the legal world these days, although not all lawyers fit this stereotype. I've encountered several types of lawyers. Lazy Lawyer. Snake Lawyer. Liar Lawyer. Smart Lawyer. Workaholic Lawyer. Ethical Lawyer. Jerk Lawyer. Most lawyers are some combination.

My least favorite lawyer to deal with on the other side of the table is the Lazy-Snake Combo. He makes my life miserable on a daily basis because I'm always doing his work for him, and he's always misrepresenting the truth and picking a fight, which means I have to work twice as hard and charge my client twice as much to document every conversation and respond to lots of nasty letters. I've gotten good at responding to nasty letters. I just make sure I lace them with lots of kind words, including "Thank you in anticipation of your cooperation." Contrary to public opinion, smart, hard-working lawyers usually don't have to be jerks.

We pride ourselves at the firm in having the highest ethics and in outworking and outsmarting the other side. Like anyone in a new job, I remember feeling unprepared and even insecure as a summer intern. I had met my match. The good news? It humbled me, which was long overdue. And it gave me a passion for excellence and a work ethic that I never would have developed on my own. I'm blessed to work with people who are smarter than I, which usually makes me look good to my clients.

The bad news? Making partner was like climbing Mount Everest. I look at the young lawyers at the bottom of the climb and I don't envy them.

The road to partnership was like being on a treadmill that keeps getting faster and faster. Even though Devoted Mommy was in the midst of bearing children, I didn't have time to second-guess myself. Instead, I kept my lawyer cape on and convinced myself, "Just run one more mile." I'd finish the mile and Lady Lawyer would say, "Just run two more miles, then it will be over." Some people just quit. But how could I quit when I'd come all that way? If I stopped, I'd lose my spot in the race and have to start over. So I kept running, even though Devoted Mommy was exasperated.

Even if you've never been on the partnership track at a large law firm, you can probably relate to applying for a new position, reaching for a promotion, or even getting your degree or job training while you're trying to simultaneously raise a family and be the best mother you can. Something has to give, but the Superwoman within defies reason and your adrenaline just keeps going and going. I'd put the average working mom up against the Energizer Bunny any day. Who needs batteries? Something inside of us won't give up, because the thought of starting over is all the more exhausting. So while some days we want to throw in the towel and wrap ourselves in our mommy capes and take a long nap in a fetal position, instead we keep pressing on.

Saying No

Like me, most working mothers can't say the word *no*. Our brain is thinking, *I just can't take on one more thing*, but our mouths just won't cooperate, especially at work. As much as we try, we just can't seem to articulate that necessary but difficult two-letter word. Why are we asked to keep taking on more responsibility? It's easy to understand. We're running on lethal doses of adrenaline and so good at multitasking that everyone just assumes we can take on more. And more. Sassy Shelly kept hoping she'd get fired during the days her company was still giving good severance packages, but she just kept getting more responsibility. Finally, she decided she was going to *try to get fired.*

She delegated, refused new work, and even refused to travel after she had her twins. But everyone knew she was an expert multitasker and highly competent, and as much as she tried she just couldn't fake ineptitude. So she continued to work, although she passed up a few promotions along the way. Her boss actually accused her of getting pregnant with twins just to avoid working on the biggest deal of the year. Why is it that employers too often take shots at working mothers when they know we are vulnerable—like when we're pregnant? Sassy Shelly has thick skin, and she fired back at her boss with some choice words of her own.

Like Sassy Shelly, I'm always asked to take on more responsibilities at work. Shelly keeps telling me I just need to start screwing things up on purpose, then I won't get any more responsibility. "Oh, I'm sorry. I thought the deadline was next Monday, not this Monday." Or, "What I meant to say is that I'm totally unreachable tomorrow. I know we had a meeting scheduled, but I've decided to take the day off."

I just don't have the guts. In this economy most of us can't afford to lose our jobs, and even Sassy Shelly isn't trying to get fired anymore. Besides, I actually like being Lady Lawyer, and I'm always preaching to Nick about doing your best.

Not being able to say no at work always gets me in trouble at home. The other weekend, I had a business trip unexpectedly cancelled on a Friday. When I announced to the family that I was staying in town, Doug and the kids immediately planned a weekend camping trip. It was one of those perfect windows of opportunity, which are few and far between. The surest way to have a chaotic week at work? Just plan some quality time with your family. If we had planned the camping trip in advance, my workload would have tripled, and the trip would have been cancelled. Sometimes unexpected windows are the best I can hope for, and I have to be prepared to make my escape on short notice. The plan? I would slip out of the office before lunch, put on my mommy cape and never look back until Monday morning. Then I remembered—I had an important 3:00 p.m. conference call. How could I possibly leave the office early?

Did I cancel the call? Of course not. I had already said yes. What was I going to say? That Lady Lawyer had gone camping for the weekend? Most of my clients don't know that I'm into camping, and I'd like to keep it that way. It would ruin my image. "No" was out of the question.

So, did I tell my family that I couldn't leave the office early? Of course not. How could I say no to my children who had barely seen me all week? They were so excited to go camping, and they didn't want to wait. This is where technology enters the picture. For working mothers, technology is both a blessing and a curse. The blessing, of course, is that we can be two places at once, allowing Devoted Mommy and Lady Lawyer to coexist. The curse? It just enables us to keep saying yes when we really need to draw some boundaries. Instead, technology helps me push the envelope.

Doug had his doubts that I could pull it off when I told him about the call. I explained to him that this wasn't the typical group of friendly clients—this was an intense group who would not tolerate the usual background noise in our family vehicle. It was crucial that we arrive at the campground before the call so that I could find absolute peace and quiet. Under no circumstances could I take the call inside the chaos of our car.

You guessed it—after getting out of town late, hitting weekend traffic, and stopping for multiple bathroom breaks, we were still driving at 3:00 p.m. The campground was poorly marked, and Doug had apparently taken a wrong turn. At 3:01 I completely freaked out and said to him, "Stop the car, now!" I opened the car door before he came to a complete stop, jumped off on the side of the road, and started to dial. Unfortunately, just when I need it most, technology backfires—we were out in the middle of nowhere, with no mobile coverage. I kept trying to dial with no luck. Looking up, I saw an old farmhouse about fifty yards away, and I started to run for a land line. An elderly woman with poor hearing and a stern look stood outside. "Excuse me, ma'am, but I was wondering if I could use your phone? You see, I have a conference call and I'm not getting any cell phone coverage out here."

She continued to stare.

As I approached her, she started to explain that she was hard of hearing, so I repeated myself. Then I noticed that she happened to be holding a cordless phone in her hand, so Lady Lawyer seized the moment, grabbed the phone out of her hand, and started to dial. At this point, she started scolding me and said, "You better not make any long-distance calls!" So I called my secretary, Loyal Larraine, on the firm's toll-free number and explained the situation. Loyal Larraine is always lecturing me about how I can't say no, but fortunately she knew I was in a panic and saved the lecture for later. She quickly covered for me and sent an urgent email to my clients, explaining that I was "traveling" and outside of mobile coverage, but that I'd be getting to a pay phone as soon as possible. Loyal Larraine is used to this drama.

Doug found the campground in about twenty minutes, and as soon as I spotted a pay phone I grabbed my briefcase, put on my lawyer cape and, again, jumped out of a moving vehicle. I quickly spread out my legal papers in an old phone booth and started my call—at least it was quiet and no one would have to know I was actually camping.

Later, Doug asked me why I constantly put myself through these fire drills. One of these times, I'm going to surprise him and actually say no. He's not holding his breath—he knows my track record.

Like when I was a brand-new partner and my then-managing partner asked me if I would like to be in charge of hiring. "How would you like to spend several hundred hours a year meeting and greeting law students, attending recruiting receptions and social events after hours, conducting interviews during your already-crammed workday, and running our hiring committee for no extra pay?"

I said yes, of course.

I enjoy spending time with law students. During our interviews I like to ask them what motivates them. The answers vary. Personal challenge. Intellectual drive. A competitive spirit. Lack of other alternatives. None of them says money. I'm sure a few of them are lying, but their responses generally play into my theory that most lawyers don't go into law for the money. Most students have a few questions for me as well, like "How do you have a life and practice law in a large law firm?" This is my favorite question to answer because I have a canned answer: "Three children. Three maternity leaves. I'm not divorced" (not a proper subject of discussion during interviews, but I throw it in anyway). "My kids and husband actually like me. I smile a lot. I exercise at lunch. And I even make time to do *pro bono* work."

It sounds convincing, but some candidates see through this response. So they ask me, "How do you really do it?" My standard answer? "I pray a lot, and I maintain a sense of humor." I'm lying in part. Lady Lawyer's prayer life is virtually nonexistent, but I probably do pray more than most lawyers, which counts for something. And it's getting harder and harder to maintain a sense of humor, especially dealing with all those Lazy-Snake Combos. But on most days I still remember to laugh.

I never got into law for money anyway. Don't get me wrong—now that I have three kids, college savings plans, and a hefty mortgage, I'm pretty much saddled like the rest of America, but I can honestly say that I have never been motivated by money. Sure, sometimes it's about doing the right thing, but the real truth is that Lady Lawyer is on a power trip. I've had this discussion with my law partner, Harvard Bill.

Most people are motivated by money, pleasure, or power. Jesus called it the lust of the eyes, the lust of the flesh, and the boastful pride of life. Most lawyers, including me, are motivated by power—otherwise known as the boastful pride of life. Bill agrees, except he doesn't quite process it in biblical terms. He's one of those intellectual agnostics, and I like to quote him the New Testament just to make him nervous. He tells me point blank, "You're never going to convert me to be a Christian." At least he doesn't blame me for trying. We both have a good laugh when Lady Lawyer turns into Fundamentalist Lawyer. She can be quite entertaining.

Clients and Good Works

Just like there are different kinds of lawyers, clients come in all shapes and sizes. Intense Client. Rich Client. Needy Client. Skeptical Client. Lawyer Client. Lawyer-Hater Client. Vindictive Client. Party Client. Macho Client. Cheap Client. Reasonable Client. Crazy Client.

The easiest client to deal with is probably Lawyer Client. I realize this seems completely contradictory to everything I've said thus far, but truth be told, it's easier dealing with your own kind. Lawyer clients are usually predictable. The worst kind of client, of course, is the Lawyer-Hater Client. Unfortunately, this is an ever-growing segment of the population. I'm at the point in my career where I really don't want these clients at all, regardless of what they might pay me. I once had a Lawyer-Hater Client come close to assaulting me and decided at that moment that some things are more important than money, like my life. I charge extra for getting assaulted.

I was recently speaking to a group of MBA students at a secular university, and they would not stop peppering me with questions about morality and the law. "Just because something is legal, what do you tell your clients when it's not the right thing to do?" I responded, "I give my clients legal advice, I don't tell them what to do or what not to do." The students were surprised. They also weren't satisfied. I tried to explain to them that my job is to tell clients what they may do within the bounds of the law and give them legal options. I am not a decision maker. My job is to advise what's legal.

But the students kept coming back to a different question—why don't I feel the need to give my clients moral advice? If not me, then who?

I couldn't stop thinking about this after the class. Most of my clients are ethical, but morality rarely enters into the equation when I give legal advice. Have I allowed myself to completely divorce law from morality? As a Christian, don't I hold myself to a higher standard?

In the book of Ephesians, the apostle Paul explains that "we are God's workmanship, created in Christ Jesus to do good works, which God prepared in advance for us to do."[2] In other words, even when I'm wearing my lawyer cape, I am supposed to be doing good works. In fact, God even prepared these good works in advance. Pastor Eric recently explained that the Greek word for *workmanship* is actually *poiema*. It's where we get the English word *poem*, and it is often used in Scripture to refer to God's creative activity. Pastor Eric went on to explain that our good works are supposed to be lived out as "poems," and God is writing His words on our hearts, minds, and souls so that we can give the performance of a lifetime. This gave me a new perspective on work. If God prepared my work in advance, it must have some spiritual purpose.

Sometimes, even Lady Lawyer tries to take this mandate of good works to heart. Last year I started representing indigent mothers who are rehabilitated drug offenders. Most of them have all but lost parenting rights, often because of abandoning their children for a lifestyle of drug abuse. My first client, we'll call her Lisa, hadn't seen her son for almost a year—since she had gotten out of prison. And even though she had stayed clean and followed the court's drug rehabilitation program, she wasn't able to convince the court she could be a fit mother. My job? To help her win back her son. Some people ask me how I can do it. "As a mother, how can you in good conscience help a mother regain her parenting rights when she abandoned her own children just to get high?" My answer? I'm a mother. Lisa's son is the same age as Nick, and it broke my heart just thinking about the pain she was feeling being apart from him. Despite her mistakes, she still loved him and wanted a second chance. I've always believed in second chances, and judging her is not my job.

Besides, I've never met the perfect client.

Speaking of perfect clients, I've given some thought about what it would be like to have Jesus as my client. I like to picture Him walking into the firm's lobby in His robe and sandals. The receptionist would probably call security. Most of our clients dress in business attire and don't have long hair, but there's really no formal dress code for clients, as long as they can pay our rates.

Assuming Jesus could make it past security, He would still have to get past the financial performance worksheet and new client intake procedures. I don't think He had much in the way of a financial portfolio or other assets, so this could be a problem. Then again, He arranged for His disciples to get money out of a fish to pay their taxes, so I assume He could find a creative way to pay His lawyer. Actually, I don't think I could bring myself to charge Him. I just know He would be my favorite client, and that would be worth much more than my billable hours. I think He would want Lady Lawyer to be tough but fair. And I don't think He'd make Lady Litigator settle just to avoid a fight, especially when I'm dealing with Jerk Lawyer who is completely unreasonable. He could tell me when Liar Lawyer is bluffing. And He could also tell me when Lazy Snake is going to strike. He wouldn't complain about my hourly rate, He wouldn't try to assault me, and He'd even understand if I said no to go on a camping trip. What more could I ask for?

Most of us wish we could change something about our workdays, and most working mothers, like me, know our jobs aren't perfect, but we're still thankful for our chosen professions, and we work diligently so our children will appreciate the value of hard work and develop a strong work ethic. Sure, maybe we need to start saying no, but the experience and opportunities that come with saying yes can make us better at our jobs and even help us to be better mothers.

Sometimes when we're reading together at night, Nick and I read the parable of the ten talents, and we both agree that neither of us wants to be the guy who buries his talent in the ground. I go on to explain that most days I really enjoy my job, because I'm being the person God created me to be and trying to do my best. Isn't that all God asks of us?

THREE

It Takes Children to Make a Mommy

> Pour out your heart like water before the face of the Lord. Lift your hands toward Him for the life of your young children.
>
> Lamentations 2:19 (NKJV)

Doug and I had been married for nine years and there was no good time to have a baby. After I graduated from law school, I wanted to have "time" to settle into my career before children entered the mix. I remember the day I found out I was pregnant. I cried. I was completely terrified. As the youngest sibling, I had never cared for anyone else—everyone always mothered me. I never had pets, and every plant I'd ever tended had shriveled and died. Until then, I had never even entertained the thought of taking care of anyone other than myself.

I was just hitting my stride in a fast-paced, demanding legal career. A baby now? What was I thinking?

It was too late for regrets. Like it or not, I was going to be a mother. And soon.

My pregnancy with Nick was uneventful—the usual morning sickness (extending into the afternoon and evening), weight gain, short temper, and mood swings. Everything seemed perfectly normal.

Sometime during the eighth month of pregnancy it dawned on me that I had forgotten to sign up for birthing classes. I kept putting it off, thinking I'd do it next month. Finally, Doug and I decided to show up for a class. After we settled in and moved the chairs in a circle, a dozen expectant parents went around the room talking about the names they had chosen, the color of the nursery, and all the planning they had done for a new arrival. Doug and I felt like we had just shown up to the prom in T-shirts and tennis shoes. We didn't have a name, didn't know the sex, and hadn't decorated a nursery. I have always liked surprises, especially good ones. After all, there's no reason to buy a bunch of clothes if you don't know the gender. And why decorate a nursery with a bunch of goofy wallpaper when something neutral will serve you well for years to come, particularly when it comes time to sell?

Just when we thought the class couldn't get worse, it did. We all moved to the floor and the instructor turned off the lights and put on freaky music and told us to start our breathing exercises. I could barely see Doug, but I knew he wouldn't last long. It takes him about two years to warm up to most people. This was a little much, even for me. He gave me the signal and we made a quick exit, no questions asked. *We can rent a video at the library,* I told myself.

At my last checkup prior to delivery, I still hadn't rented the video. I was thirty-eight weeks, and Nick was breech. We were hoping and praying that Nick would turn. My sister Encouraging Amy, who birthed all of her children at home through a midwife, had me doing exercises, standing on my head, and observing other old wives' tales. She tried her hardest to convince me I could do it: "Just stand on your head another thirty minutes, and we'll pray the baby turns."

When you have four older sisters who have all birthed children before you, you are going to get your share of unsolicited advice.

In oversimplified terms, I have two pairs of sisters: my right-brained sisters—Mona and Janie—and my left-brained sisters—Marybeth and Amy. I consider myself quite lucky to be surrounded by such balance.

Mona, my Firstborn Sister, is proud to be the oldest. She's organized, driven, put-together, and responsible. She's always trying to convince me that I am really a firstborn prototype, despite my birth order, because according to her research the gap between Janie and me caused the family birth order to repeat itself and turn me into her firstborn twin. I listen attentively but know deep down that I will never be that organized or responsible. Just ask Self-Employed Stefanie or Sassy Shelly about my study habits.

Janie, my other right-brained sister, is also known as my Blonde Sister (Mona went blonde after she turned forty, so that doesn't count). My girls have fondly nicknamed one of their Barbie dolls "Aunt Janie" and I often hear them say that Aunt Janie is in the bathtub, or Aunt Janie doesn't have any clothes on again. Don't let the blonde jokes and Barbie image fool you—Blonde Sister is one of the most sensible, put-together women you'll ever meet in your life. She and Firstborn Sister keep their homes as if they just came off the cover of a magazine, and they're always showered on the weekends (unlike me) and have perfect hair and makeup, increasing the hygiene standards for the rest of us.

Not surprisingly, my right-brained sisters told me to follow the advice of my doctor and take as many drugs as I needed for childbirth. I can still hear Firstborn Sister saying, "Natural childbirth is for the birds. Don't be a martyr." Blonde Sister fully agreed, "You're crazy if you don't take the drugs."

My left-brained sisters, Marybeth and Amy, rave about natural childbirth. Marybeth, my Artist Sister, has a heart that is bigger than Texas and a sense of empathy that is unmatched. She's the closest thing to a flower child in our conservative family, and she and Encouraging Amy nursed their children longer than my father will ever know (at least longer than I'm allowed to write about). Encouraging Amy is always the first one I call when I'm in a crisis. Most importantly, she's a woman of prayer, which is why I've got her on speed dial, even though I know I'm going to hear all about her latest nutrition kick or home remedy. She and Artist Sister tried hard to persuade me to have a natural delivery with no drugs—"You don't want all those drugs to affect the baby, after all."

Of course I was torn. Before going to that last checkup, I hadn't decided yet if I would follow the advice of the right-brained or left-brained sisters. It was a toss-up, and I figured I'd just play it by ear. Besides, I had a couple of weeks before delivery. Right now, I was more worried about stopping in my office first to get ready for a deposition later that day. I can still picture that ugly gray suit I was wearing. By my third pregnancy, the pants would rip and the front would be stained from breast milk. When you are in your last weeks of pregnancy and you feel like you're the size of a house, anything that fits will do. Who wants to spend more money on maternity clothes when you're ready to pop?

I decided to walk, a fifteen-minute stroll from my office, to what I thought would be an uneventful checkup. If I was lucky, maybe I would be dilated. All of my sisters agreed I shouldn't get too anxious with my first delivery, so I was playing it cool. To my surprise, after a quick exam, the doctor immediately recommended that I proceed with a C-section. Nick's position had shifted, and labor could be high risk. I went back to the office and started crying. I wasn't ready to deliver a baby. I hadn't even cleaned off my desk. So I proceeded to do what most expectant mothers do twenty-four hours before delivering their firstborn: I put on my best poker face and went to take a deposition.

I was in the midst of contentious litigation. Opposing counsel, a Jerk Lawyer, looked at me straight in the eye prior to the deposition and said, "When's the baby coming?"

I lied, "In a couple of weeks." I couldn't let him see that I was weak and vulnerable. I could cry later. Now, it was time for Lady Lawyer to take care of business. For Lady Lawyer, there are certain advantages to being pregnant. I find that most witnesses are eager to spill their guts and make damaging admissions to a pregnant woman. I appear sweet, innocent, and harmless. All I want is the truth, the whole truth, and nothing but the truth. A pregnant lawyer is a sheep among wolves. My motto? "Be as shrewd as snakes and as innocent as doves."[1]

By the time I finished the deposition, I had regained my composure and hadn't let my guard down. I couldn't give Jerk Lawyer that satisfaction. But I was still unprepared. And scared. Even though I had the advice of my older sisters, I wished I hadn't skipped all those birthing classes. I had gotten comfortable wearing my lawyer cape. Would a mommy cape even fit?

Lessons from Mary

When I look at the birth of Christ I am comforted by Mary's lack of planning. It doesn't appear she attended birthing classes or decorated a nursery. She didn't have a birthing coach, and she was far away from family and friends, traveling to Bethlehem. The amazing thing is that God had prepared her.

I had read the story of Mary and Elizabeth since I was a child but only recently was struck by God's complete brilliance in using the birth of John the Baptist to prepare Mary for her own labor and delivery. When the angel Gabriel visited Mary and foretold the birth of Christ, Elizabeth—John the Baptist's mother-to-be—was already six months pregnant. Mary went to visit Elizabeth and stayed with her three months.[2] Six plus three is nine, so Mary must have stayed for John's birth. Assuming she did, she would have watched and learned about labor and delivery firsthand from her older cousin Elizabeth. Like me, Mary had a relative to teach her the ropes. I'm not sure if Elizabeth was a left-brained or right-brained "sister," but I know she had Mary's best interest at heart. So Mary didn't have to attend birthing classes or rent a video. How else would a young virgin in the middle of Bethlehem know how to give birth with an inexperienced husband in a stable?

I had grand visions of going through labor and delivery without fear. I would welcome the pain and have a quick and easy delivery where *I* would be in control, not the doctors. Okay, maybe deep down I knew I would take the drugs, but a scheduled C-section is not what I had in mind. Have I mentioned that I hate hospitals? I've represented too many doctors in litigation, usually when they got in trouble, and it's not pretty. The Lawyer-Hater Client who almost assaulted me? You guessed it, a doctor. Now I was completely at a doctor's mercy, going under the knife. Doug couldn't watch.

Then Nick entered the world. Becoming a mother was the most exhilarating experience of my life. Nothing else even comes close. My mommy cape not only fit—it was warm and cozy, and quickly became my favorite. I had entered the special yet mysterious club of motherhood. Mary and I had a new bond.

Every Christmas, when I get out the familiar nativity scene, I stop for a moment and hold Mary in my hand. I wonder if childbirth was exhilarating for her, or whether she was too scared and unprepared to enjoy the moment. Was Joseph freaked out like Doug? I can't wait to ask her someday what it was like to birth Jesus in a stable. Where did she get the swaddling clothes? Did she bring them on the journey, or did she borrow them from the inn? Did Jesus cry like most babies, or are the words to "Away In a Manger" really true? Crying or not, like most mothers, I'm sure she treasured every moment. Too bad she was so far from home. She couldn't call her mother and say, "It's a boy," even though Gabriel had already spilled the beans. And the next few months had to be equally difficult, caring for a newborn while traveling around on a donkey.

Day-Care Drama

I love newborns. The best part about them? They don't talk back. Those first few months, Nick screamed most of the time he wasn't sleeping, but I didn't mind. A screaming baby was a welcomed break in Lady Lawyer's routine. Besides, he was *my* screaming baby, and I knew our uninterrupted time together would be short. I got an occasional call or two from the office, but for the most part I left my work behind for nearly sixteen weeks and focused completely on Nick. We were inseparable.

Leaving Nick to go back to work was like ripping my heart out. Everyone told me it would be hard. I can't say I was surprised. It just hurt more than anything I could remember. What were my options, anyway? I was five years into a successful legal career, had a baby, and found myself leaving him in the arms of a stranger. I cried a lot those first days. So much that sometimes I forgot to pray.

As an associate at the firm, I had little flexibility. Fortunately, Doug did. We decided that he would work at home in the afternoons while Nick napped, and we would hire someone to watch Nick in the mornings. It seemed like a good plan. How hard could it be to find someone to love and care for my precious newborn? After screening about fifty candidates over the phone and meeting about fifteen women in person, I selected a young but experienced nursing student, Sleepy Sally. (I didn't realize she was sleepy until after I hired her.) When I first met her, she seemed smart, energetic, and had good references. She'd be with him for only about four or five hours a day. What could go wrong?

I took some comfort in the fact that my office was only five minutes from home. My first day back to work, I waited until lunch to call and check on Nick. There was no answer. I left a couple messages, thinking that Sally had possibly taken him outside. To satisfy my curiosity, I decided to drop home myself. Sally's car was still there, so I walked in, looked around, but still saw no sign of Sally. I put on my mommy cape and flew straight to Nick's room, relieved to see him lying in bed, sleeping. But where was Sally?

After searching the house several times I finally found her, sleeping in our attic. Devoted Mommy wanted to smack her, but I pulled myself together, woke her up, and asked her to leave. I was so hysterical I couldn't breathe. After she left, I couldn't stop shaking. *Why didn't I have a hidden camera? How could I be so stupid? Of course she was sleepy, she was working two jobs while trying to go to nursing school. What was I thinking?* I would have to quit working. I could never trust anyone again. Doug came home to calm me down. I was too upset to fire her. Lady Lawyer is a master at firing *other* people's employees, not her own. Especially not when it involves her children. I could go ballistic. So I made Doug do it.

Now it was back to the drawing board. I never prayed so hard in my life. Come to think of it, I prayed pretty hard before I hired Sleepy Sally, but something obviously went terribly wrong. Wasn't God listening? Why didn't He try to stop me? I dusted off the names of the candidates I had screened and previously rejected. I came across my notes on Big-Hearted Betty: "Old, experienced with babies, talks too much, a little crazy." I decided to call her back. Big-Hearted Betty has a gift with babies. The first time she held Nick I knew she would care for him like her own grandson. I didn't hire her right away because I thought she was too old, and I was concerned about her crooked knee. So I made her show me she could walk up and down our stairs while carrying Nick. Nick didn't seem to mind about the crooked knee. He just wanted love and attention. It's just like God to answer my prayers with the unexpected. I just didn't think He would answer them with an elderly woman with a big heart (not to mention a big mouth) and a crooked knee.

Round Two

About a year and a half later I became pregnant with Anna. Had I been thinking with my head, I would have waited another year. After all, I would soon be up for partner, and having another child would likely delay my admission. Instead, I followed my heart. Making partner could wait. My biological clock was ticking.

Everything is easier the second time around, or so I thought. I had forgotten how sick I felt being pregnant. Plus I had Nick to take care of, and my law practice had become even busier and more demanding. Lady Lawyer was on the cusp of making partner, and the treadmill just kept getting faster and faster. I couldn't stop now.

Anna arrived in the middle of the summer, two weeks late. I was miserable and hot, but it gave me much-needed time to finish my work and actually be prepared the second time around. No more scheduled C-sections for me. My left-brained sisters didn't even have to twist my arm. I was going to have Anna the old-fashioned way. No one was going to cut me open again if I had a choice.

In the end, I took the epidural but avoided the knife. It was well worth the wait. When the doctor proclaimed, "It's a girl," I burst out crying and called my parents. Anna was their thirteenth grandchild. After a string of seven boys, they were more than ready for a little girl again. My father has never been the same. This is the same man who ruled with an iron fist, chased our boyfriends away, and gave his daughters the claw around our necks with his huge hands when we got out of line. His grandsons can't even raise their voices or he scolds them for being wild and unruly. He is nothing but tender with my girls. Never mind that they chase the boys, jump on the furniture, scream in high-pitched voices, and have broken my mother's favorite lamp five times. To my father, they are like gentle flowers that can do no wrong.

Anna was indeed my flower child. My living room looked like a funeral parlor after she was born, with all the bouquets from clients. Things at work seemed to be going quite swimmingly. I would check my email on a regular basis and enjoy Anna in between her naps. Clients called me at home on an as-needed basis. It would be difficult to return to work, but at least I had Big-Hearted Betty. I could forgo the dreaded day-care search and just focus on enjoying Nick and Anna. Anna was a great sleeper, and our household was soon in a smooth routine. We moved out of the city and into the suburbs. What could go wrong?

Big-Hearted Betty's crooked knee had gotten worse, and surgery became inevitable. She decided to schedule surgery right after Anna's birth so that she could have a full three months to recover and be ready to care for Anna and Nick by the time I headed back to work. It seemed like a perfect plan.

Just a few weeks after having Anna, I got a call from Big-Hearted Betty. She had been injured in a serious car accident and would take time to heal. She would be in no position to take care of a two-year-old and a newborn any time soon. The knee surgery would be rescheduled around other medical complications. We both cried. Big-Hearted Betty wanted nothing more than to take care of Anna and Nick; I wanted nothing more than to have my children cared for by a trustworthy, kind woman who would love them as her own. But we both knew I would have to move on. Back to the drawing board.

Most working mothers have been stuck without child care on short notice. It's like having an uneasy feeling that aches every time you breathe. Some of my friends are lucky enough to have family nearby to cover the unexpected, but for those of us with no family in town, a backup plan is hard to come by.

Again, I screened close to fifty candidates and interviewed a dozen or so before finding Jill. Jill came to us with top-notch references and experience with several local families. She was organized and professional. She was also expensive. Doug and I didn't know if we could afford her when we first met her, but we bit the bullet and hired her.

It was one of our better decisions. Jill took care of the kids until she and her husband adopted a child of their own, and she has been like family ever since. God knew I just couldn't handle any more day-care drama.

The Third Time's a Charm

The year after Anna was born, I made partner. It was as if a huge weight was lifted off our shoulders. Doug and I could breathe again. I don't know why it meant so much to me, but it did. I knew that everyone had made a sacrifice for my career, especially Doug, and I was just glad to have the hurdle over.

Everyone, including Doug, was surprised when I became pregnant again. I had a healthy boy and girl, and a busy legal practice. Why complicate matters? It would be one thing if I stayed at home, but why would I want to continue working full time to barely keep my head above water caring for three children? I must be crazy.

I am crazy indeed. Crazy about my children. I'd have three more if I could, but in my heart I knew Abby would be my last. As soon as I got home from the hospital after Abby's birth, Doug packed up my maternity clothes and sent them to the Salvation Army. Never mind that I had nothing that fit me for the next few months. I could take a hint. At least he waited until she turned two to pack up her baby clothes and send them away. I cried my eyes out. I still haven't forgiven him.

Nick had been early, and Anna had been late. Abby was just about right on time—a couple days early to be exact. The week prior to her birth I had client negotiations an hour away. I desperately wanted to complete the project before going on leave. Doug and I had an argument as to whether I would drive out of town so close to Abby's birth, and we finally agreed that my law partner, Harvard Bill, would accompany me. I hadn't told anyone that the doctor had told me at an appointment earlier that day that he would not give me forty-eight hours before I would go into labor. Sometimes, too much information is a bad thing. Especially when Lady Lawyer has work to do.

Abby was cooperative. She waited for me to return from negotiations and came the following weekend.

Who said anything about maternity *leave?* The nurses rolled their eyes when I took my BlackBerry into labor and started answering emails from the hospital. When Abby was three weeks old, my managing partner called to see if I wanted to meet with a potential new client. Lady Lawyer could barely fit into her pants (breathing would have to be put on hold, especially since Doug had discarded all of my maternity clothes), but I welcomed a night out of the house and quickly squeezed back into my lawyer cape.

Several weeks later, Lady Lawyer next hopped on an airplane … again … for another potential business venture. My breast pump barely made it through airport security, and one of my partners ignorantly offered to carry it for me. "What's this, anyway?" he later asked. He gave me a blank stare when I told him he had been carrying a breast pump around the airport.

In less than twelve weeks, I was back in the office every day, sooner than I had planned. It was just easier to get things done from work instead of trying to do it all from home. I don't know how Sassy Shelly or Self-Employed Stefanie (or for that matter any working mother) can work from home. It's virtually impossible.

Don't get me wrong; it was just as hard to leave Abby to return to work—and in some ways it was harder, knowing she would be my last—but we soon got into a routine and I was thankful to have a loving caregiver for her in my absence. Besides, had I stayed home any longer, Jill would have fired me. God never intended for two women to run the same house.

I don't know any mother who hasn't struggled with leaving her newborn to return to work. I always second-guess myself. Sometimes I wonder, *Am I really providing what's best for my children? Wouldn't they be better off if I was with them all day?* I could feed them healthy food, limit TV intake, read them stories for hours, potty train them early, keep them on a strict schedule, nap them religiously, sign them up for "mommy and me" classes, keep them away from sick kids, and screen their playdates. (Ok, I'm probably exaggerating a bit, and I would certainly skip the "mommy and me" classes, but you get the point.) Most days I feel as if my best hours go to client meetings, conference calls, and court appearances. Devoted Mommy is exhausted by the end of the day, and Doug and the kids are stuck with my leftovers. What's wrong with this picture?

I don't have the answers. And I'm always leery when someone tells me she has it all figured out. I just know that it never gets easier. It's just not natural for a mother to give up control. As my kids get older, I think they need me *more,* not less. It's one thing to delegate nap schedules and diapers. But as they get older, it's going to get harder to delegate homework projects, the Internet, video games, peer pressure, and after-school activities. I'm going to need to install a hidden camera just to monitor my teenagers from the office. So as I pull out of the driveway each day, I try to remember that God is in control—not me—and I ask Him to keep the children in His care until we are safely united again. And I cherish the support of other mothers who encourage me every step of the way.

Lessons from Laura

My niece, Level-Headed Laura, is one of those mothers. She is always sending me encouraging notes about being a passionate mother while having a career. I recently got to watch Laura go through the struggle of returning to work after birthing her second child, Harrison. My heart goes out to her as I watch her juggle it all with grace and confidence. It's never easy. I always save her notes. This is one of my favorites:

> *I really appreciate the way that you were so real and straightforward with me at Grandma's about how it is HARD to leave your kids, even when you enjoy your job and know it is valuable too. It is so refreshing to hear someone just say it. Often, I feel like my working-mom friends want to hide that they cry when they leave in the morning. Anyway, I wanted you to know that you made me feel so much better knowing that I am not insane for enjoying my work and wanting to be home, too. And it also made me feel liberated to cry in the morning and then be okay in the afternoon.*

Level-Headed Laura, ten years my junior, has always been more like my younger sister than my niece. Just after she and Cole got married (and started to think about having children and balancing her career as a teacher) she would ask me, "Aunt Susie, how do you do it?" I'd give her my standard response, but also explain it's not easy.

We were all elated to find out that Laura was expecting. I waited with eager anticipation to watch Firstborn Sister be the first to have a grandchild of her own.

After Laura's first ultrasound, we knew things were not going to unfold as planned. On a cold Thanksgiving Day we will never forget, we gathered around the table and cried and prayed as Laura and Cole explained to us that their daughter was going to have some special needs.

As Laura's ninth month approached, the doctors were amazed at the baby's incredible strength, despite her rare medical condition. Laura carried her for nine full months, and on Easter morning, Aubrey Rose was born into the arms of Jesus. Rose, a family name, taken from our grandma, Rose D'Ercole, symbolized the great determination and passion of the women in our family. Although Laura was physically and emotionally drained, she returned to work shortly after Aubrey's passing just to say good-bye to her students.

She could have ridden out her sick leave. Certainly she had every right to say, "Hey, I'm recovering from losing my firstborn, not to mention childbirth. I need some time alone, and I'll see you all next year." Everyone would have understood. Instead she wanted closure. She could have pushed people away. Instead she chose community.

I've never returned from maternity leave without the joy of a child to come home to after a long day's work. What do you say to your colleagues when they ask you how you're doing? How do you go home to a quiet house, and how do you forget about losing your baby when your body is still recovering from childbirth?

I know Laura will never forget the pain. In many ways, she wouldn't want to. But I also love to see her with Harrison, knowing that he is a special gift from God and she treasures every moment. So I pray that Laura would be strong as she balances being a passionate mother with being an excellent teacher. Leaving my children to go to work is never easy, but nothing is more rewarding than coming home to your children and being reunited after a long day's work. Yes, my mommy cape is probably the hardest cape I wear, but I wouldn't trade it for anything.

FOUR

The Daily Grind

Be still, and know that I am God.

Psalm 46:10

My day typically begins at 7:00 a.m. I know what you're thinking: This is awfully late. Most mothers of young children begin their day at some painful hour like 4:30 a.m. Been there. Done that. My get-out-of-bed time does have its exceptions, such as when I have to get into the office early, catch a morning flight, run with my neighbor Emily, take care of sick kids, or help Nick finish his homework that we forgot to do the night before. But most days, I relish every extra minute of sleep.

Once I get out of bed and hit the ground running, there's no turning back. In a matter of one hour, I have to shower, dress, get ready for work, eat breakfast, make breakfast for the kids, help Anna pick out her clothes, dress the kids, change Abby's diaper, check backpacks for lunches and homework, check the calendar for carpool duty and other schedule changes, and get out the door. If we have carpool duty, that means we have to leave at least five minutes earlier to pick up Reed and Jack, so I really should have gotten up at 6:55 a.m. Most mornings, I'm cutting it close.

It's humanly impossible to get all of this done in one hour. But I try. The morning is the one time I readily admit I couldn't do it without Doug. He does circles around me. By the time I roll out of bed at 7:00 a.m., he has already showered, eaten breakfast, read the paper, and had his coffee. (Mind you, I single-handedly put the kids to bed the night before while he passed out in his La-Z-Boy at 8:00 p.m. watching ESPN.) He's pretty handy to have around in the morning.

Even with Doug's help, I still have to cut corners. The shower is the first thing to go. I can pull my hair back in a twist, spray on some perfume, and no one will know the difference. Showers are overrated, and most Americans are too obsessed with hygiene. I learned that in college traveling through Europe. Blonde Sister disagrees, but even she can't argue that I'm pressed for time in the mornings. Besides, I much prefer an evening soak in the bath after everyone is in bed. Breakfast is also optional. My own breakfast, that is. I wouldn't be a decent mother if I let my children go without breakfast, but I can always grab something on the go. I used to get a toasted bagel with cream cheese, or better yet, a moist cranberry scone. Bagels and scones unfortunately ended with my low-carb diet, so I settle for some granola and a few nuts.

On a good day, it usually takes me twenty minutes to dress Anna and do her hair. The first dilemma: She can't decide what she's going to wear. She has one shirt she likes, "butterfly shirt," that she rotates with pink and brown pants. Butterfly shirt is ripping because we wash and wear it five times a week, but Anna doesn't care. She often prefers to get butterfly shirt out of the dirty clothes rather than wear something inferior. If I'm lucky, she'll settle for her leopard tank top. Unfortunately, it's usually the middle of winter when she wants to wear leopard tank top, and her teachers will ask me again why she's not wearing clothes. My answer? I don't have a good one. I just pick my battles. I'm going to spend most of my day fighting with Jerk Lawyer and trying to calm down Crazy Client, so I really don't want to have a fight over leopard tank top.

Unfortunately I'm not very spiritual in the morning. It's not that I haven't tried. I've set my alarm, bought devotionals, and even taken early showers. Nothing seems to work. I've heard lots of sermons about the importance of "quiet time" in the morning. I can't argue with the concept. It makes perfect sense: Start your day out right, spend time in meditation and prayer, and order your priorities. I even heard a pastor say that he has yet to meet a "serious Christian" who doesn't spend at least an hour in study and prayer every morning. Obviously I need to get with the program. But by the time I've gotten myself and the kids out the door, I've forgotten to pray. Besides, it's time for me to change from Devoted Mommy into Lady Lawyer. Lady Lawyer is too busy to pray.

The Commute

I have always had a short commute. During my first five years of practice, we lived in the city. Even after having Nick, I was bound and determined: I would not flee to the suburbs. I would be an urban mother with urban children. Then, when Nick turned one, both of our neighbors were robbed at gunpoint and I forgot my urban ideals. We ran to the oldest and stodgiest suburb we could find and never looked back. The good news is that even on a heavy traffic day, my commute is still only twenty minutes.

A short commute certainly has benefits. I spend less time in the car and get to see more of my kids. But a short commute also has its challenges. It's short. Sometimes, too short. Every New Year's Eve, I resolve that I'm going to use my commute for prayer and quiet time. But by the time I check my voice mail and return a few calls, my commute is over. Lady Lawyer is in full gear.

My car has turned into my second office. When Nick turned five, he went to Safety Town and learned a bunch of things about safety, including what your parents should and shouldn't do while driving a car. The result? "Mom, you really shouldn't be talking on your cell phone while you're driving. It's dangerous." And I actually paid for him to go to Safety Town. I wanted him to learn safety, not turn into the family sheriff. Aren't they supposed to learn about bike riding, stranger danger, and poison control at Safety Town? Who inserted the material on parent cell phone use? Not a working mother. At least not one with my kind of job.

For most mothers, multitasking is not optional. It's a matter of survival. Asking me not to use my phone on my commute is like asking me not to breathe. I have to make the most of every moment, short or not. Then again, I'd probably be making the most of every moment if I used my twenty-minute commute just for quiet time and turned off everything else.

Sometimes I ask myself what I would do if I had a long commute. I'd probably feel guilty for spending more time away from the kids. I'd probably pray more in the car, but I'd get home later, be more exhausted, and might even have less patience. For now, I'll stick with my short commute. Every once in awhile, I just have to remember to turn off my phone and savor a few minutes of solitude. Once I walk into my office, I'm lucky to have an undisturbed moment in the bathroom.

The Day That Never Ends

One good thing about a busy legal practice is the days go fast. Incredibly fast. By 5:00 p.m. I wonder where the day has gone. I still have calls to return, emails to read, and deadlines to meet. I try to turn my laptop off and pack my briefcase, but my desk is like a vacuum, pulling me in with all its force, and my chair is like a magnet. I can't get up. Lady Lawyer and Devoted Mommy start to wrestle. Devoted Mommy can already hear the kids calling and they're starting to get hungry. Lady Lawyer can hear her clients complaining tomorrow if they don't get a return call tonight. The struggle continues until Devoted Mommy prevails. As soon as Lady Lawyer completes her last email and hits the send button, Devoted Mommy shuts down her laptop and runs for the door ahead of schedule. It feels like escape from Alcatraz.

But we haven't seen the last of Lady Lawyer. Just as I pull into my driveway at 6:05 p.m. my cell phone rings. I almost don't answer it, but it's the president of my largest client. This can't be good.

Prior to leaving the office, I had emailed him the "final draft" of an agreement. He now needs another draft of revisions, and he needs it immediately.

He starts to explain his latest crisis at the same time I have pulled into my garage. My children have already spotted me. I quickly put my phone on mute, blow a few kisses to the kids, and run into the house, thinking it will be a short conversation. Of course, I'm wrong. Given that it's a beautiful summer evening and the kids are playing outside, I assume they will enjoy the fresh air and leave me alone in our home office. Again, I am wrong.

I've come to learn the art of carrying on a phone conversation by utilizing the mute button frequently. My clients call me for legal advice and sometimes I actually have to talk back. Most attorneys, including me, talk too much. Using the mute button forces me to listen.

By the time I need to unmute and speak to my client, my three children have all followed me into the office. Where is Doug when I need him? I spot him out the window, but he's already cutting the front lawn. I motion for him, put the phone back on mute, and yell, "Help! I need your help. I'm talking to a client." But he can't hear me because the mower is too loud and he assumes I'm just trying to make conversation.

I have no options, so I panic. Desperate for some childproof space so I can talk to my client, I run outside and into the middle of the street and unmute my phone. By this time, my client figures out that I have arrived home, and I make some joke about the background noise. But my client didn't call me to hear background noise. He needs the agreement now, and if I can't help him he'll find someone else who can. After all, there's no shortage of attorneys these days. By this time, Abby is screaming at the top of her lungs, heading for the street. My neighbor graciously intercepts her while I finish my phone conversation, and Doug continues to cut the grass. I end my conversation promptly and head into our home office to finish the agreement.

Why didn't I just stay in the office? I'll tell you why. It's simple: I'm a mother. I need to see my children and they need to see me. Nick wants to tell me about school, Anna wants to show me what she's been practicing in gymnastics, and Abby just wants me to hold her. I so desperately want to give them my undivided attention, but I can't. Not yet. First I need to end my workday. Easier said than done.

Just when I think I have things under control, my laptop freaks out. I'm starting to have "issues" connecting to the network from home. Unfortunately the last version of the agreement is on the network and, no, I did not save a copy on my hard drive. I call our firmwide "help desk" and get put on hold. "All of the help desk analysts are busy right now assisting other callers. Your call will be answered in the order it was received. Thank you for your patience." What patience? I have only so much patience, and I reserve it exclusively for my children. Mothers need patience. Lawyers don't. Speaking of patience, the kids have followed me into the office and all of them are screaming for my attention. Nick and Anna are still arguing about who gets my attention first. Abby is still screaming because she just wants me to hold her. I can't hold her because I don't have a free hand.

I finally break through to an analyst named George. A human being at last—I'm in business. George explains in greater detail than I care that my router isn't recognizing my wireless connection. I have no interest in understanding the problem; I just want it fixed. I can barely hear him as he walks me through a series of connectivity drills. This is what I get for leaving the office early. I wasn't thinking like Lady Lawyer. She needs to do a better job of keeping my mommy cape away from the office. Devoted Mommy needs some serious boundaries. For all I know, she probably sabotaged my laptop.

As George continues to walk me through the drills, Abby is screaming so loud that I can barely hear him. I don't press the mute button. The mute button is reserved specifically for clients. I don't have to worry about impressing George and the firmwide technology geeks. In fact, the louder my kids yell, the more they try to help me just so they can be rid of me and my screaming children. Sometimes screaming kids can work to your advantage.

I remember the days when I used to work at home and actually found it productive. When I first started practicing law, Doug and I would try to have a late dinner together most evenings. If I couldn't get my work done in the office, I'd bring it home and get a few things done after dinner. After Nick was born, I found myself leaving the office early just so I could have some quality time with him before he went to bed. Firstborns, of course, always go to bed early, and I'd put him to bed around 8:00 p.m. and still have time to do some work at home.

With three kids, all that has changed.

By the time I complete the agreement, it's 6:45 p.m. I still have to properly greet the children, have dinner, do homework, give baths, put the laundry away, unload the dishwasher, return emails in between baths and stories, read stories, do prayers, and finally tuck three kids in bed. Doug always tells me I need to put them in bed earlier—that I shouldn't fall for one more book or yet another glass of water. He's probably right. Why do I feel as if I have to read to each of them individually? Why can't I simply read one story to the group, throw up a few prayers, and turn off the light? I'm probably just trying to make up for the fact that I've been gone all day. Even Doug doesn't argue with my intentions. He just hates to see me totally and completely exhausted, and he knows that, chances are, by the time I put them to bed I'll have more work to do into the evening.

By 9:00 p.m. I'm simply too tired to work. At this point, I wish I would have started my day earlier to pray. Now, I'm too tired to pray. I go from being too busy to too tired. Sometimes I wish God would just hit me over the head or shake me upside down to get my attention.

The Gentle Whisper

Sassy Shelly and Conservative Jen—another friend from law school, who is married to Bleeding-Heart Brian—decided to read through the Bible with me last year. Conservative Jen has four children—four seems to be the magic number for my friends—and she retired from the practice of law to stay home with her firstborn almost eight years ago. I'm always jealous that she gets her kids in bed by 7:00 p.m., but I also realize that most days she works harder than I do. She and Bleeding-Heart Brian are two of my favorite people, except I try to stay away from them during most political elections, when they have their share of marital discord. They make Doug and me look completely compatible.

A lot of folks are surprised that Sassy Shelly is involved in Bible study, but she's always eager to learn something new, and like Conservative Jen and me she's ready for some girl time at the end of a long day. So the three of us meet for Bible study on Wednesday nights after our kids go to bed, and we make no apologies for moving at a snail's pace. Right now, we're stuck in Kings. We've been in Kings for about three months. Now, the Old Testament can be pretty tedious, but Kings comes alive when I read about the prophet Elijah. Elijah is a wild man. He's always on the run, being fed by ravens and taunting all the evil prophets of Baal. At one point, he is running from the wicked King Ahab, and he hides in a cave. God tells him to go stand on the mountain, because the Lord is about to pass by. So Elijah listens. Next comes a mighty wind, then an earthquake, and then a fire. But no sign of the Lord. Finally, the Lord appears in a gentle whisper. It's a good thing Elijah was listening or he might have missed it.

Some things never change. Even though I'm not running from King Ahab, it's still hard to hear a whisper. I'm always looking for God to appear in the obvious places. Sometimes I even get angry at Him when He doesn't show up. Never mind that I haven't been listening. I usually do all the talking, and unlike me, He's a good listener.

Nick likes to ask me, "Mom, have you ever heard God speak?"

"Yes, dear, God speaks to us in all kinds of ways."

"But, have you ever heard His voice? Has He ever spoken to *you?*"

This is a more difficult question. I give Nick a canned answer and explain that God speaks through the Holy Spirit and uses the

Bible, prayer, other people, and circumstances. But this isn't what he's asking. He wants to know if I have ever heard God's audible voice. I can't say that I have. But I try to explain that sometimes, when I am really quiet, I can actually hear Him speak to my heart. Just like the gentle whisper.

So far, Sassy Shelly's favorite part of the Old Testament is the story of Samuel, right before the book of Kings. Her oldest son is named Sam, an unexpected blessing that changed her life forever, and she especially likes the verse that says, "I prayed for this child, and the LORD has granted me what I asked of him."[1] Nick also loves the story of Samuel, so we read it together and he listens with wide eyes as God calls Samuel—a young boy like Nick—not once, but three times before the priest Eli finally realizes that God is calling Samuel by name. The fourth time, Samuel is actually ready. Instead of running to Eli, Samuel responds, "Speak, LORD, for your servant is listening."[2]

Pastor Eric recently explained that even though Samuel grew up in the temple, he didn't recognize the voice of the Lord without some help. Even Samuel took time to become a good listener.

Like Samuel, I need some help recognizing God's voice. Some nights, I need to hear His voice more than I need the sleep. So I stay up late, I listen, and I finally pray. And then I start writing. Chances are, I'll probably skip my shower in the morning. I'm trying to be a good listener, but it's still not easy. I live in two worlds, and both of them consume me. There's no gray in my worlds; it's black or it's white. Like a switch, I'm on or I'm off. In a matter of minutes I go from my corner office, navy suit, and high billing rate to sibling rivalry, poopy diapers, and soiled clothing. I want to listen at some point in between, but I'm exhausted, and I'm not sure where to begin. At the end of my long day, Jesus comforts Devoted Mommy, gives grace to Lady Lawyer, and understands when I just collapse in bed.

FIVE

Superwoman Takes On School

> Trust in the LORD with all your heart and lean not on your own understanding; in all your ways acknowledge him, and he will make your paths straight.
>
> Proverbs 3:5–6

When you're busy pretending to be Superwoman you don't have time to read instruction manuals. Like the manual that explains the complicated demands that most schools place on parents. Actually, I'm not sure such a manual exists. Most working mothers feel like we're already behind the eight ball. Many of us are not able to pick up our kids from school, so we don't get the take-home folder until the papers have mysteriously disappeared into the far corners of our homes, and we frequently mix up dates, forget assignments, and miss last-minute changes—like the notes that say "please send your child a packed lunch tomorrow for the field trip" or "every child should wear pajamas on Friday for the party." I'm always worried that my children are going to suffer because of my lack of involvement. I want to "trust in the Lord with all my heart" and put my children's school experiences in God's hands, but it's always a struggle.

It all started in preschool. Preschool mothers have a way of making simple things complicated. At the end of Anna's first year of preschool, a letter went out to all of the parents expressing concern over preschool snacks. Just about every preschool snack is taboo these days. A vocal group of parents were concerned that the kids were eating junk every day, so they put a task force together to "study" the issue. All parents were asked to complete a survey with three options: (1) Let the kids continue to eat junk; (2) Pay more tuition to the school and have the school provide a healthy snack; or (3) Have a parent committee organize parent-driven healthy snacks. You guessed it, I voted for option 2. The last thing I need is another school-related responsibility.

The votes had been cast, and option 3 was the clear winner. So the next fall, a memo went home to all the parents with elaborate instructions on snacks. No nuts, no trans fats, no carbs without protein, only good protein, a fruit or vegetable every day, not too much sugar, and not too much mess. Snacks were to be individually wrapped, fruit was to be washed, and teachers were to always wear gloves in the classroom when serving snacks. Just reading the memo made me exhausted. I opened our refrigerator and quickly realized I would have much work ahead.

When it's Anna's turn for snacks I usually don't remember until the night before, after the kids have gone to bed. Doug usually sees "preschool snack" on the calendar, and we both panic. I look feverishly for the preschool snack calendar and can never find it. I think I may have thrown away that memo with the instructions. So I immediately send Doug to the grocery store to pick up some boxed raisins and cheese. Who can argue with raisins and cheese? It's certainly an improvement over goldfish crackers, my standard snack the year before. Actually, the year before I usually forgot snack when it was Anna's turn. In a fit of guilt, I would buy eight bags of goldfish and take them to preschool the next day as a "backup snack." When it's Anna's turn to bring snacks, she also gets to be line leader. It's tough to be line leader when you don't have any food to feed your friends.

Kindergarten

When Nick entered kindergarten I embarked on a new journey that only a mother of grade-school children can understand. I was completely unprepared. There's no instruction manual for parents of kindergarteners, and even if there was, I wouldn't have time to read it. I hate instruction manuals anyway. I'm the kind of person who skips the first page of directions and goes straight to the last step. I can usually figure it out myself.

Besides, I had already been through preschool. You would have thought that two years of preschool would have prepared me. Not so. Kindergarten is much more intense. One difference, at least in our school, is that the teachers are really in charge. In preschool the parents are in charge. Of course, the parents are paying for their children to attend preschool, and money talks. In our public grade school, parents can talk all they want, but at the end of the day we're all at the mercy of the school. Like everything else, there are things you can do to influence the school, something I would learn later in the process.

It all began on a cold February morning, waiting in line to request Nick's kindergarten teacher. Kindergarten sign-ups are first come, first served—parents who arrive first get preference on teacher selection. Fortunately, this madness occurs only for kindergarten. The doors open at 8:30 a.m., and I arrived at 8:00 a.m., thinking I was ahead of the game. I was late. One class roster had already been filled. Parents were asked to sign a list noting their arrival time. You could tell I was a first-timer.

Nick still made it into kindergarten, even with my preference of teacher. After kindergarten screening, kindergarten orientation, the annual school-supply sale, and the kindergarten welcome ice cream social, he was more than ready to take the plunge. He counted the days down until the first day of school. I cried my eyes out. It was worse than his first haircut.

At our grade school, the teachers have to discourage parents from volunteering. Nick's kindergarten teacher wisely told the too-eager parents that she wanted the first few months of school to get to know the kids, without mom or dad. In other words, "Stay out of my way, and junior will be fine." I could live with this. I don't have time to volunteer anyway. She already had two aides and a student helper, so Nick would get plenty of attention.

By mid-October, the parents were chomping at the bit to get into the classroom, so she finally put a volunteer schedule together.

I emailed her and told her I would like to come into the classroom once a month, but that my schedule changes every month and is completely unpredictable. I suggested that we email some workable dates back and forth and gave her a couple of upcoming possibilities.

"I'm out of town the week of November 10, but the following week I have a window the morning of November 18 (although I just offered that date to someone for a deposition), and I can volunteer on November 20 but I would just need to leave a few minutes early so that I could get to our partner lunch on time."

I never heard back. When the November schedule arrived in Nick's Friday folder, I wasn't on the schedule. I certainly didn't blame his teacher. My secretary and I have a hard enough time keeping track of my schedule; I can't expect Nick's kindergarten teacher to figure it out.

Fortunately, Nick is a good student and he gets along fine in the classroom without me. When I was growing up, parents rarely appeared in the classroom. My parents came to every ballet recital and cheerleading meet, but I was on my own in the classroom. I completed my own homework, walked to the bus stop alone, and never brought treats on my birthday. Things have changed, especially when it comes to birthdays. In addition to bringing a snack, most kids bring goodie bags for everyone in the class. These goodie bags have homemade snacks, small toys, and craft projects. The days of a sucker and pencil are over. The average parents will go broke before buying their own child a birthday gift.

Parent-teacher conferences have also become a production. The night before Nick's first conference, I could barely sleep. Nick has always been good at home, but what if he had been acting out at school? Since I never volunteer, what if I got caught by surprise? Or worse, what if Nick's teacher didn't think he was special? Quiet, compliant children like Nick never get any attention. I felt sick just thinking about it.

The morning of the conference, I arrived a few minutes early. I had purposely scheduled an early slot at 8:30 so that I could get into my office as soon as possible. At 8:40 I was still waiting—the 8:00 conference was apparently running late. The reason? Nick's teacher was being interrogated by another parent. Another lawyer parent. I decided to eavesdrop since the door was open.

"We've tried to work with Marilyn at home, but she just doesn't seem interested."

"I understand, but after a day of school, some kindergarteners just aren't ready to engage again."

"We're concerned that she's not being challenged enough at school."

"Well, I can start giving her additional homework if you would like."

More homework? Nothing like robbing a five-year-old of her childhood. If Marilyn starts doing more homework, Nick will be left behind. Isn't homework supposed to start in something like seventh grade?

It was 8:50 a.m. by the time they wrapped up the homework discussion. It looked as though I was going to miss my 9:00 conference call. Oh well, it wouldn't be the first time. I quickly sent my client an email. "Tied up in important meeting but will call as soon as possible." I wasn't lying. This was my most important meeting of the day.

I was completely relieved to hear that Nick was doing well in school, had no issues, played well with others, and generally thrived in the classroom. What more could I ask for? I certainly wasn't asking for more homework.

Even though Nick gets along fine without me, he kept asking me when I was going to volunteer in his classroom. Finally, I told him I would come on his birthday. The days leading up to his birthday I was completely paranoid that I would have to cancel unexpectedly. A client would have an emergency, a federal judge would order me to appear in his courtroom, or I'd have one of those busy days where I would completely forget until school was over. I emailed Nick's teacher in advance to let her know I'd be coming. She told me she would stick to the regular volunteer schedule, but that I was welcome to show up in the classroom anytime. In other words, she too had doubts about my schedule.

The day of his birthday I was thrilled to be free and clear of client emergencies or court appearances. I decided to wear jeans and take the entire day off. When I put jeans on in the morning, my kids know something is different. Nick was so excited he could barely contain himself.

We made chocolate cupcakes the night before and filled the goodie bags. I planned to arrive in his classroom at 9:00 a.m. sharp, when the regular parent volunteer arrives. When I arrived at 9:00 a.m., not one but two parent volunteers had already settled in. Neither had met me before.

"Oh, you're Nick's mom. Doesn't your nanny usually pick him up?" I smiled and bit my lip. I was there for Nick, not to impress the suburban mafia.

By the time I helped oversee a craft, it was 10:00 and time for the kids to go to art. Nick's teacher told me we would sing "Happy Birthday" to Nick at 11:00, when the kids returned to the classroom. This was my opportunity to get coffee. I hadn't had my double-tall, nonfat latte and the coffee shop was only a block away. This was also a prime opportunity to bribe Nick's teacher. I asked both his teacher and her student helper if they wanted coffee since I was going on a coffee run. You would have thought I'd offered them both a trip to Hawaii. When you volunteer only once a year, bribing the teacher is essential. Those other mothers may show up every week, but how many of them buy her coffee? I knew she was likely to be Anna's kindergarten teacher in a couple of years, and then Abby's. I would be buying coffee for many years to come.

Since that coffee run, Nick's kindergarten teacher and I had a new bond.

Toward the end of the school year, I asked Nick's teacher how I could go about requesting that he be placed in the appropriate first-grade class. She gave me a cold stare. The coffee had apparently worn off. She told me that, while I was welcome to visit the first-grade classes, parents are strongly discouraged from requesting a first-grade teacher. She promptly ended the discussion. If I had questions, I could talk to the principal.

Unfortunately, I don't have time to sit and observe first grade. Most mothers get their information the old-fashioned way. The mafia. I thought long and hard about approaching them. I also thought about what they would require in return. A potluck casserole? A committee designation for Family Fun Night? An afternoon campaigning for the upcoming levy? I got scared just thinking about it. So I decided to use a few connections of my own.

Enter Lady Lawyer

Lady Lawyer had just given a modest but noticeable gift to the law school, so I called one of the law professors to ask her opinion of the first-grade teachers since she has two sons just senior to Nick. Most parents are very opinionated about their children's teachers, and she was no exception. She had the first-grade teachers ranked by enthusiasm, teaching style, creativity, and overall classroom management. The good news? I didn't have to consult the mafia. I had all the information I needed.

Lady Lawyer decided to write a letter to the principal. Spiritual Mommy thought about letting it go, praying about it, and resisting the desire to manipulate the system. After all, God is in control of first grade, isn't He? I've never been very good at giving up control when it comes to my children. Lady Lawyer was overpowering. So I tossed up a few prayers and wrote the letter. I sent the principal a pleasant email, introducing myself, complimenting Nick's kindergarten teacher and the wonderful experience he had had at the school. I then proceeded to explain the type of first-grade teacher I wanted for my son and ranked the first-grade teachers in order of preference. I ended the email by including "Esquire" after my name, with my law firm signature line. I can't stand it when other lawyers do this. It's downright tacky to use my professional status to wield power at the grade school. But when it comes to my kids, I'll break my own rules.

So I rationalize. If I can't be there volunteering, I can at least use what influence I have to get Nick the best teacher.

I had so much fun volunteering for Nick's birthday that I decided to do it again the last day of school. I even signed up to plan the last-day-of-school party. The day before the last day of school, I emailed Nick's teacher to see what I needed to do. Apparently, the party had already been planned, and I had deleted the emails telling me what to bring. In any event, she was pleased to have another set of hands and told me I was welcome to show up. Nick was thrilled, and I took the entire day off work.

On the last day of school, the kids have a swim party and meet their first-grade teachers. Not only had Nick been placed in the class I had requested, he was placed with two of his very best friends. Nick was beaming. Over half the kindergarten mothers were present on the last day of school, most of them eager to find out about first-grade teachers. I overheard several remarks about Nick and his friends being placed in the same class with the school's top-notch first-grade teacher. "I wonder how that happened," one mother said to another. The mafia was in an uproar. Another mother mentioned under her breath but loud enough to be heard that it was complete taboo to request a teacher, and the principal never honors such requests. I bit my tongue and smiled.

First grade is even more complicated. Nick brings home a red homework folder every night. He usually has nightly homework in reading and basic math. Spelling homework is always assigned each Monday and due on Thursday. By Friday I'm completely exhausted. I don't remember having homework in first grade. If I did, I can guarantee my parents didn't have to sign a nightly homework log.

How will I ever manage when Anna starts kindergarten? By then, I'll be inundated with second-grade homework. The good news is I won't be a rookie. I'll arrive at kindergarten registration by 7:00 a.m., and Anna will get the best teacher. I'll buy more coffee, write more letters, and pray more. Being a mother of school-aged children is something I don't take lightly. As much as I make fun of the mafia, it's my own insecurity and guilt that drives me to make fun of women I don't know, who have time I wish I had and get to spend more time and energy with their kids at school than I will ever know. I can't argue with their intentions. The mafia and I have something in common. We're all trying to figure out what's best for our children.

I should have written *The Idiot's Guide to Grade School for Parents* instead of this book. It would be a best seller and I'd be a very rich woman. The problem is I don't think I could write such a book with any degree of passion. There's simply no formula. Every time I think I have it figured out, the rules change. Kindergarten may be about face time and volunteering, but first grade is about homework and carpool. I can only guess about the expectations of second grade, let alone the years to come.

I'm against formulas anyway, just as I'm against instruction manuals. So I decide to just live day by day and pray.

Dear Lord, help me to trust You to take care of my kids at school. Forgive me for always trying to take matters into my own hands and battling with the system for control. Show me how to support my kids at school, even when I can't be with them. And help me not to resent the mafia. I confess my own insecurity and pray You would take away the nagging guilt of wanting to be two places at once, and show me that You are in control, even though I'm not. Amen.

SIX

Superwoman Goes to Hollywood

> Man looks at the outward appearance, but the LORD looks at the heart.
>
> 1 Samuel 16:7

I grew up in a church that embraced the fundamentalist traditions of no drinking, no swearing, and no dancing. "We don't drink, smoke, or chew, or go with girls who do." Ironically, the only time I experimented with alcohol as a teenager was with my church youth group. It was a short experiment. I got sick, woke up in a fog, and quickly decided this was a "thou shalt not" worth adhering to. As for swearing, no one in my family used curse words, including me.

But no dancing? I couldn't deal with that.

I have always liked the story about King David dancing before the Lord. His wife, Michal, apparently didn't agree. She scolded him for "disrobing in the sight of the slave girls," but David didn't seem to care what anyone thought about him except God Himself.[1] I like that about David. Now I realize that David wasn't dancing in the nightclub scene—he was dancing before the Lord in worship. I just genuinely appreciate his spirit of freedom.

Late-Night Fashion

Too often Christians are caught up worrying about what other people think and, as a result, they never make it out to the night-clubs. Not me. I have always liked the nightclub scene. People are fun to watch, and it gives me a chance to dance.

During college I went on a mission trip to Eastern Europe with a group of other students who, like me, always figured God wasn't against dancing. Our primary goal was to build spiritual bridges with other college students in an emerging, post-communist society. And, yes, some of our best spiritual conversations were in the nightclubs. Now that I am married with three kids, I don't get out to nightclubs much. Shocking, I know. But every once in awhile I muster up the nerve to go out, just so I can see what's going on out there. Each time I do, I learn a few things.

Like the last time I went out in Hollywood. We had a partners' meeting in nearby Los Angeles, which is where a bunch of lawyers get together, eat and drink too much, and talk about how much money we can make for years to come. The first night of the partners' meeting, a group of us decided to go to this new club in Hollywood. The club is too exclusive for the average Midwestern lawyer to get into, but we had a few connections.

Jock Jill took a cab with me to meet the rest of the group, and some blond-haired, six-foot-three bodyguard named Chris let us in the back door. It's the kind of club where you can't find the back door unless you know what you're doing. We didn't know what we were doing. Chris spotted us from the inside and opened the door. Midwestern lawyers are easy to spot in Hollywood. Jill had a pretty swanky outfit on, but Midwestern swanky has long been out in Hollywood.

I was overdressed. I had clothes on. The new style in Hollywood is apparently no pants. I knew that underwear had long been out, but no pants? This was news to me. I'm exaggerating only slightly. There were several women in the club who wore long shirts with nothing but their birthday suits on the bottom. I am not beyond staring. I'm a mother with two daughters, after all, and I need to be informed. I dared to think, "I wonder what their mothers would say?" Even Superwoman wears underwear. Doesn't she?

Once I got over the initial shock and stares, I felt very sorry for these underwearless women who were wearing no pants. It just made me sad. Then I thought of Anna. Ever since she turned two, Anna has resisted clothing. She's always hot, which is one of the reasons she's constantly taking off her clothes. She doesn't like to wear underwear. It's too restraining. I thought this was just a phase, but apparently Anna has embraced West Coast fashion.

I'm already having visions of Anna in Hollywood and it's quite disturbing. So I pray, "Dear Lord, please don't let Anna grow up like those women in Hollywood with no underwear and no pants."

What can I do to make sure it never happens? It's already happening. Just prior to my trip to LA, she was playing in the snow in her bathing suit and snow boots. And that's in the middle of winter, below freezing. If she ever moves to a warm climate, she'll probably give up clothes altogether. I know my neighbors must wonder what kind of mother I am. And unlike King David, I tend to worry too much about what other people think.

My mother always quotes from Proverbs with confidence, "Train a child in the way he should go, and when he is old he will not turn from it."[2] I just don't have my mother's level of faith, but I wish I did. I wonder if I can quote that verse as a guarantee. Even if I can, there's no guarantee kids won't rebel when they're young. It says when they're *old* they won't turn away. So do I have to wait until my kids are old to see if they turned out? I might be dead by then. I'll have to admit, since I've become a mother I've placed a heightened value on my own life. Hollywood is proof that my children are going to need me, at least for moral censorship, for years to come. Lawyers can be replaced. Mothers can't.

Inner Beauty

Like me, Anna loves to dance. It's innate. She first started asking me if she could go to dance class back when she was three. I found a ballet program for three-year-olds but decided to put off the inevitable. She still kept asking. I finally gave in after she turned four. Ballet class is the only time each week she doesn't refuse to get dressed. Besides, you don't have to wear underwear with a leotard and tights. Being a former ballerina, I can't argue with her. Underwear only gets in the way.

Anna is also consumed with her appearance. Like her hair. She was having one of her three-going-on-thirteen tantrums, and she burst out that she didn't like her curly hair. Through her sobbing, she proclaimed in a fit that her hair looked "terrible." It nearly broke my heart. I told her that her curly hair is beautiful, that Mommy has curly hair, and that God made her hair curly. She continued to cry.

I have no idea how this happened. How did my young, beautiful daughter become so concerned about how she looks? It's unthinkable. Immediately I think it must be my fault. I wear too much makeup. She sees that I spend too much time primping, getting ready for work. I really need to trade in those high heels for some sensible flats. I'm gone too much. I should have never left her overnight on business when she was only three months old, even if she was with my mother. If she and I could spend more time together, she'd never feel insecure.

I thought it was just Anna, but then Abby started. Before she could walk, she started wearing my high heels around the house. One of her first words was "shoes." She and Anna constantly play dress-up and princesses, raiding my makeup and jewelry. What's a mother to do? Of course I can tell my girls that "God looks at the heart," not outward appearances, but these words seem hollow when everything around them is threatening to rob their innocence.

I try to read Anna Bible stories before bedtime. I even bought her the Princess Bible, but she still prefers to read about the Disney princesses. Ariel is her favorite. Unfortunately, Ariel is no role model. Forget obedience to parents or nurturing her God-given talents and inner beauty. She's in love with Prince Eric and will put everything aside, including her own soul, for his admiration. So she disobeys her father and makes a deal with an evil sea witch to give up her only talent, her voice, for a man she has met only one time. And I'm trying to teach my girls to love God first, resist evil, and resist men, at least until they complete graduate school.

Lord, I'm really struggling here. My girls need a role model, please help.

Where am I going to find a suitable role model for my young daughters these days? I have always admired the woman in Proverbs 31, but it's just hard to find a modern-day, "cool" role model who lives by the virtue "[c]harm is deceptive, and beauty is fleeting; but a woman who fears the LORD is to be praised."[3] These words mean so much to me, now that I am a mother of girls. My own parents raised five girls. No one told me it would be this hard. And Ariel is no help.

The pressures on girls today are simply unbearable. Every time I shop in the little girls' department I am stunned by the prominent display of training bras. Call me old-fashioned, but I really don't think my preschoolers need to be concerned about their breasts. And these stores aren't even subtle about it. Sure, society has always been focused on outward appearances, but I believe the bra messaging has recently spun out of control. I remember shopping for bras with my mother as a preteen, a very modest and private experience. We had to ask the lady in the lingerie department for her "assistance," and she brought us training bras from behind the counter, prepackaged in cardboard boxes. Things have changed.

I shudder just thinking about the teenage years. I think back to my own youth. You could have told me that beauty is fleeting until you were blue in the face. I wouldn't have given up big hair, eyeliner, and miniskirts to save my life. Yet my own mother was patient. The fear of the Lord was modeled, not forced.

Looking back at old photos, I wish someone would have told me to lighten up on the eyeliner. Eventually, I abandoned big hair and miniskirts, but not overnight. I'm too old for miniskirts—at least that's what Doug tells me. The big hair is genetic, but nothing a little hair gel can't fix.

My mother always showered her daughters with compliments. We would stumble out of bed with bad breath and bed-head. Before we could open our sleepy eyes, she would stroke our hair and say, "My, I really like your hair that way," or, "You know, I don't even think you need makeup." She never told us we were too fat or too thin, and she didn't even bother to tell me when my eye makeup was too heavy or my jeans were too tight. I got to figure that out on my own. Instead, she was never negative about our appearances and always said, "You're just right the way you are." The result? I developed a terrible ego that eventually matured into a solid sense of security. At least I never felt the need to display myself in public or go without underwear.

It seemed to work, so I might as well try it with Anna. Every day I tell her she is beautiful just the way she is. I'm not lying because she is literally the loveliest expression of God's creation I have ever seen. (Abby is still too young to rival her, but will be equally beautiful as soon as she grows some hair.) I tuck Anna in bed, then I tell her that even though she is beautiful, the most important thing is to have a beautiful heart. Sometimes I quote Proverbs 31 out loud and beg God that she will grow up to value inner beauty. Anna gives me a big smile and she's asleep in about thirty seconds.

Anna has announced she wants to be a rock star when she grows up. She is crazy about Hannah Montana, and I can only hope that Miley Cyrus won't disappoint the millions of little girls who are looking up to her. Especially my little girls. I cringe every time the Britney Spears' tune plays on the Barbie keyboard as Anna and Abby sing in unison, "I'm not that innocent." I remember when Britney was young and innocent. Such a bright, young, talented star....

I confess I haven't prayed for Britney Spears or Miley Cyrus. I know I should, but I have my hands full at the moment. I'm too busy worrying about Anna wearing underwear and Abby's obsession with high heels. I thank God for showing me the women in Hollywood as a reminder of just how fragile my little girls are. Something good always comes out of my experiences in nightclubs. So I keep telling Anna the most important thing is to be beautiful on the inside, and I keep praying that she and Abby will grow up to be women who fear the Lord. I want to be a Proverbs 31 woman, a true role model for my children, but so many of us with daughters are still so scared for them because we know the pressures we felt and sometimes gave in to as girls. And we know the stunts we pulled and got away with, before the days of GPS tracking, of course.

So even though it's her dream, I really hope and pray that Anna won't become a rock star (unless God speaks to me out loud and tells me it's His will). The pressures on girls today are just unbearable. What mother would want her little girl subjected to yet the additional pressures of Hollywood? And what mother doesn't want her little girl to always be sweet and innocent?

Too much pressure for one little girl.

SEVEN

Superwoman Goes to Church

> But in fact God has arranged the parts in the body, every one of them, just as he wanted them to be. If they were all one part, where would the body be? As it is, there are many parts, but one body.... There should be no division in the body, but that its parts should have equal concern for each other.
>
> 1 Corinthians 12:18–20, 25

I can still remember a former pastor's words. He was explaining how evil the world would get in the last days, quoting with authority from the Olivet Discourse: "At that time many will turn away from the faith and will betray and hate each other.... Because of the increase in wickedness, the love of most will grow cold."[1]

He went on and explained that we are obviously living in the last days. The evidence? Mothers who put their children in day care. Forget wars, rumors of wars, earthquakes, and biblical prophecy. Day care would usher in the second coming of Christ. Why would a devout Christian woman sacrifice her children for a career, unless of course her heart had grown cold? Never in all of human history have mothers abandoned their children for a paycheck. Not until now. Yes, there are certain "circumstances" where a mother has to work. But in most instances, mothers who work outside the home are motivated by good old-fashioned greed.

My jaw dropped and my heart sank. I could feel myself getting warm, and I felt as if everyone in the room was watching me. I was in my third year of law school, ready to launch my career at a big firm. And I wasn't exactly planning on being a stay-at-home mom. I wanted to be a top-notch lawyer *and* a devoted mother. Would the church still accept me?

I went home and read the Olivet Discourse for myself. I didn't see any mention of day care or working mothers. Was I missing something?

Doug told me not to worry about it. "Who cares what people think? What matters is what *we* think."

Actually, I was more interested in knowing what God thinks. I just couldn't hear Him. Too many people were speaking for Him.

Eve's Curse

This wasn't the first time I had heard the church take a swing at working mothers. Usually, it was in the context of Adam and Eve, a regular hot button for women and the church. I vividly remember sitting through a Bible class where the teacher explained the roles of husbands and wives, based on Adam and Eve. Adam's curse was that he had to toil in the ground. Hence, men are in charge of work, providing for the family. Eve's curse was that she would have pain in childbirth. This was figurative in part, meaning that it was Eve's responsibility for the family and children. One of the students raised her hand and stated, "I know a situation where the wife has a good job, providing for the family, and the husband takes care of the kids." The teacher responded, "I would seriously question whether the husband and wife are living out God's plan."

Did Eve's curse mean that I had to forget law school loans, courtroom aspirations, and my desire to serve God in the marketplace? I wasn't convinced. Eve may be the mother of all, but shouldn't we learn from her mistakes, rather than use them against women? Come to think of it, Eve was really at a disadvantage since she didn't have any female mentors. I can't imagine the pressure of going first. She couldn't call her mother to ask her how to know you're going into labor, or what to do when your newborn won't stop crying, or how you know your baby is getting enough milk. And she couldn't ask her grandmother to babysit the kids for the evening so she could get some rest. She had to learn everything the hard way, herself. And she must have had more heartaches than most mothers, especially when Cain killed Abel. She probably said to herself, "If I hadn't eaten that rotten apple, Abel would still be alive."

So when I hear Christians pulling out the "Eve" card, I think to myself, "That wasn't exactly the way God intended the family to function in the first place. Have you read Proverbs 31 lately?"

Proverbs 31 paints a beautiful picture of the wife of noble character, the epitome of a working mother. She burns the candle at both ends—she arises before dark, and her lamp doesn't go out at night. And in addition to completing the traditional tasks of feeding and clothing her family, she buys a field out of her own earnings, plants a vineyard, engages in profitable trading, and feeds the poor. All in a day's work.

It didn't sound easy, but at least it was possible. Maybe I could be a top-notch lawyer and a devoted mother.

I started to ask some of the young mothers in the church if they could help me make sense of how the world of law and motherhood might fit together. Reactions were mixed.

A few told me that "It will just be a few years while your kids are young," and "Maybe you can work part-time and still practice law while you have a family." One woman even told me about a woman in the church who had a law degree. She decided to edit legal books in her spare time so that she could maintain her skills while staying home with her family. After all, "What's more important, your career or your family?"

It didn't sound promising. Apparently, I had to choose between my family and my career. Spiritual women obviously put their families first. Selfish woman put their kids in day care, putting their careers before their children. Was I that selfish? Maybe my heart was not the heart of a mother. The bar seemed higher than I could reach.

I wanted desperately for other women of faith to tell me that I'd be okay. That they had walked a similar path. That they too had doubts, but in the end their children turned out just fine. But like me, everyone else had questions, but no real answers. So I decided to leave the church that told me I had to choose between being a lawyer or a mom. I just didn't want to argue about it. And I didn't want to be judged. It was easier to walk away.

Role Models

Don't get me wrong. I had wonderful role models growing up in the church. But all of the esteemed women in our church spent the best hours of their days with their children, and when the children were in school, they had time to volunteer, engage in community activities, and otherwise manage the affairs of their homes. A few of them worked full time outside their homes, for financial necessity, and we all felt sorry for them because they "had to" work.

Even outside the church, none of my close friends had mothers with careers. Some of our moms had jobs, and my own mother went to work for a retail clothing store when I was in grade school. My father always joked that she spent her entire paycheck on clothing (and it cost her more to work than to stay home) but she helped put five kids through college and found some independence in the process, even though she continued to maintain complete and sole responsibility for the domestic affairs of our home.

It's been almost twenty years since I've heard the church denigrate working mothers so passionately. But sometimes I wonder how far we've come.

Lots of women in my church work these days, but most of us still feel the guilt. It's one thing to work outside the home, but being a partner in a big law firm is a little much, even for me sometimes. Maybe I shouldn't be working in such a demanding career, and I should be spending more time at home. But please save that debate for another day and another book. The fact is, I'm working. I'm working a lot. And while I love my church, I also love my work. But I still can't seem to get connected to other like-minded women. Lots of us are in desperate need of mentoring, but we don't have the foggiest clue where or when we will find the time.

I thought about contacting my church's support group for working moms. Then I realized we don't have one. The last time I looked at the church bulletin I saw a bunch of play groups and daytime coffees. Of course a few Bible studies meet after my workday, but try telling three small kids you haven't seen all day that you are leaving again to go to church. It doesn't go over well.

That's probably why our church doesn't have a support group for working moms. There's just no good time to meet. I know I'm not alone; sometimes it just feels that way. Try billing over two thousand hours a year while maintaining a healthy marriage and family of three small children, not to mention a relationship with God, friends, and extended family. Who has time to get connected?

I used to be involved in women's groups and discipleship. And I had lots of mentors. Before I had kids.

Nonjudging Jane mentored me in college and we still keep in touch, although I don't see her very often. We live in different worlds. I live between my home and my office; I start my day early and try to wrap up by 10:00 p.m. Jane lives among college students, and her day often *begins* at 10:00 p.m. She devotes her life to helping college women know and follow God. I can barely follow God myself, let alone help three kids on the path to faith. But Jane and I still maintain a deep connection. She's always understood my heart, a rare gift in a friend. And while she's one of the most conservative women you will ever meet, she doesn't have a judgmental bone in her body. Back in college I had little if any desire to be a mother or raise children. I was bound and determined to head straight for law school. Jane cheered me on every step of the way.

Maybe you are blessed to know someone like Nonjudging Jane, someone who is ten times more spiritual than you and lives out a faith that you could only dream of. More often than not, no one wants to be around these kind of people. Why? Because whether it's intentional or not, they just make you feel like a spiritual minnow. Not Jane. Jane has a special gift—even though she is more like Jesus than any person I've ever met, she never puts anyone else down or acts like she's Super Christian. In simple terms, she's humble. Which is why she's so easy to be around.

Another thing I love about Nonjudging Jane is that I can be myself around her. I've told her how much I struggle, that I blend in with the Jerk Lawyers, that my language becomes more foul every year, and I'm hardly the model Christian mother for my children.

She still loves me and believes in me.

Nonjudging Jane always asks me to come and speak to her students about serving God while working as a lawyer. As much as I love speaking to college students, I've turned her down the last few years. Why? I don't have the time. The kids are too young to come with me. I hate to travel on the weekends. And most importantly, I don't claim to be the best role model for college students aspiring to live out their faith. What am I going to tell them anyway? Reach for your dreams, but don't be surprised if they suck the spiritual life right out of you in the process. And if you're planning to have children and work full time, brace yourself for the guilt, the stress, and the isolation that you will feel inside the church. I could lie and tell them that I have it all together, but I've never been very good at lying. So I'd have to tell them that I still haven't figured it out and regularly fall flat on my face.

It wouldn't be a very inspiring message. What would I do with Lady Lawyer? She moves left of center every day, and I'm not sure I could shut her up, especially if we're going to talk about the law. She'd probably go off on a tangent and offend everyone, and I'd get Jane in trouble for inviting some militant crazy woman to speak to a group of impressionable college students at a Christian conference.

So I've been staying home.

Lady Lawyer tried ministry once. It didn't last. Shortly before I had Nick, I connected with a group of women in my downtown who wanted to meet, pray, network, and bring in inspirational speakers. It seemed like the perfect plan. I chaired the group for almost two years and met some incredible friends. We were organized, energized, and had about fifty women meeting every other month for lunch. After about eighteen months, the group flopped while I was out on maternity leave. In addition to my role as chair, I had taken over the responsibilities of the secretary and treasurer.

After having Nick, I just couldn't do it anymore. The group soon disbanded. So I gave up.

I learned a lot in the process, and I know that, despite my fear of failure, I should probably start a new group for working moms with the support of my church. I've already had a handful of women approach me. One thing's for sure, the next time around I'll pray first, put other people in leadership roles, and make sure it's not just about me.

Coming Full Circle

I know God has a sense of humor because He keeps trying to speak to me out loud when I'm in my office. No kidding. Lady Lawyer was sitting at her desk trying to bill some hours when I received an email from a former church leader I'll call John. Yes, this is the same church that proclaimed over ten years ago that day care would usher in the second coming of Christ. Sure, it probably didn't *mean* to link Armageddon and working mothers, but I certainly hadn't forgotten its words. I felt a lump in my throat as I began to read the email. It included an apology. Totally unexpected. John told me he was very sorry for having a negative reaction to my professional goals. Not only did he apologize, he went on to say that his black-and-white thinking was wrong and a misrepresentation of the Lord. He finished the email by proclaiming, "I'm sure you had the wisdom to ignore a fool. I thank God for His grace once again!"

I was completely dumbfounded. Why me, and why now? Doug and I hadn't been part of that church in over a decade. We had left behind some dear friends and had many good memories together, but when we left, our friendships became a thing of the past. While we were hurt by the rejection, the experience had made us stronger in many ways, and time has a way of healing old wounds. Even back then, no one really knew how much I had been hurt. I probably should have told John—Doug and I were close to him and his wife and he would have listened and maybe even understood—but I just wasn't strong enough. I certainly never expected him to apologize. Especially not now. But somehow, God knew that I needed to hear his words. Like me, John hadn't figured everything out either. Like me, he needed grace.

I closed my door and wept. With my luck, one of my colleagues would knock on my door any minute and find Lady Lawyer in a puddle of tears. I just wanted to be alone and escape from my office, at least until I could pull myself together. This was just too complicated to explain to Harvard Bill or even Jock Jill and I longed to be in the privacy of my own home. I thought I was over the rejection I had felt from the church so many years ago, but the truth is, I wasn't. I had been carrying it with me too long, and I had to let it go.

I've come to realize that the church is full of imperfect people, just like me, who are trying to give their best to God and haven't quite figured out what that looks like day by day. I've also come to realize that pulling away from the church isn't the answer. Working mothers need to be part of the heart and soul of the church, and the church needs to be part of the heart and soul of working mothers. The fact is, we need each other, and God created us to live in fellowship, not isolation. Yes, it's going to take some patience and creativity—like late-night Bible studies and early morning email prayer chains—but no working mother should feel that she's not welcome inside the church. It's going to take more people like Nonjudging Jane—people who don't draw lines in the sand, but instead stand beside us as we try to be excellent workers and devoted mothers. And it's going to take more of us who are working mothers—mothers who have celebrated successes but have learned from failures—to share our experiences with other women and encourage each other as we grow and learn together.

Working mothers have much to learn from the church. And yes, the church still has much to learn from working mothers.

EIGHT

Adventures in Shopping

> Do not store up for yourselves treasures on earth, where moth and rust destroy, and where thieves break in and steal. But store up for yourselves treasures in heaven, where moth and rust do not destroy, and where thieves do not break in and steal. For where your treasure is, there your heart will be also.
>
> Matthew 6:19–21

Most of us have too much stuff. As a result, our kids have too much stuff. Sure, we try to be thankful for what we have and not hold our possessions too tightly, but it's still tough to keep things in perspective, especially for those of us who like to shop. Material possessions are not bad in and of themselves, but as Matthew 6:21 points out, hearts tend to follow treasures. As much as the kids and I enjoy shopping together—and have created some memorable and entertaining experiences in the process—I try to teach them that life is about much more than accumulating more things, and we need to be content with what we have and help those who are in need. This doesn't stop us from venturing out on our weekend shopping excursions. Starting with the grocery store.

Adventures in the Soup Aisle

I used to enjoy the grocery store. I would cut out coupons in advance, have a neatly organized list, shop the specials, and leisurely drink my double-tall, nonfat latte while strolling through the aisles, planning my next gourmet dinner. At a comfortable pace, I would get my shopping done in less than forty-five minutes. Sometimes, one of those annoying mothers with screaming children would be in the aisle next to me.

Can't you control your children? I would think to myself, *Better yet, if you can't control them, just leave them at home.*

I have become the annoying mother in the grocery store. I get those disapproving stares on a regular basis, and it's not pretty. I know the shoppers around me must wonder, *Why on earth is this woman dragging three small kids to the grocery store on a Saturday morning?* It's a fair question. Unfortunately, I don't have the leisure of sitting at home and drinking coffee on Saturday mornings while my kids watch cartoons. Don't think I wouldn't like to. Weekend Mommy doesn't have a spare moment before she has to run off to baseball practice, birthday parties, and gymnastics, so she has to get her shopping done early. And of course the kids want to come with me. They haven't seen me all week.

I tried to delegate grocery shopping once. It lasted about two months. Nanny Jill would come home with avocados that weren't ripe or meat that wasn't lean. Then I gave Doug a shot. He would get everything I *didn't* put on the list—chips, beer, ice cream, frozen pizza, nacho dip, and bacon. The perfect diet for a healthy family of five. Unfortunately, if you want some things done right, you just have to do them yourself. Especially when it comes to food. Now I really don't care if you put my sheets on backward or fold my towels in opposite corners. And I couldn't care less if my piano isn't perfectly dusted and I can even live with a little clutter. But don't mess with my refrigerator.

The four of us head to the grocery store on Saturday mornings like clockwork. I always tell Nick and Anna not to hang on the cart because it makes it terribly heavy to push with the weight of three children, but they never listen. If I'm lucky, all the child-friendly carts shaped like cars will be taken by other customers, and I can snatch a normal cart that doesn't have a steering wheel and swinging doors and the turning radius of a semi. My goal is to strap Abby into the child seat, at least for the first ten minutes, until she inevitably escapes and then we play the chasing game all over the store. She throws stuff in the cart faster than I can put it back on the shelf, and it's always the stuff that's not on my list. Nick and Anna usually can't stop laughing, which only encourages her to put more food in the cart. Her favorite? The soup aisle. We have more cans of Dora the Explorer soup than I can count.

I try to give all the unwanted products back to the cashier at the checkout, but I always end up with a few surprises when I get home.

Last week, the only surprise was a bag of raw, unsalted almonds. They're actually quite addictive. I single-handedly ate the whole bag myself because it's a sin to waste food and no one else would eat them. I had a stomachache for three days. The raw almonds still beat the multiple packs of fruit snacks or those awful colored marshmallows that are so miniature you can't even roast them over a campfire. At least the raw almonds are on the low-carb diet.

By the time I check out of the grocery store, we are pushing ninety minutes and everyone, including me, is ready to go home. Nick is complaining he's bored, Anna is doing gymnastics on the railing at the checkout line (the one that has a sign that says "no swinging on the railing") and Abby is trying to open and eat just about everything in the cart. If I'm pushing the car cart, it usually doesn't fit through the checkout aisle because the wheels are too big, so it takes me twice as long to unload the groceries, and then I have to back up the car and push it around the checkout lines and through the exit just to reload my groceries. Abby is behind the wheel, steering, and she's howling with delight. I'm ready to have a meltdown, and I swear to myself I am going to sue the makers of these carts as soon as I have the time to pull together a class action suit. I'm sure I can unite mothers of young children who, like me, have experienced the firsthand consequences of the cart and related emotional distress.

Just when I think I'm through the woods, it never fails—we always forget something on the list. But who wants to go back and get it? Not me. I've had my fill. Never mind that it's usually something we really need, like chocolate chips for the cookies I promised the kids we would make when we get home. It's just not worth another trip through the store. I've thought about asking one of the strangers around me to watch my kids for a few minutes and hold my place in line, but I've never gotten up the nerve. Most of the customers around me want to get rid of me by now, and I certainly don't blame them. Plus, I can always send Doug back to the store for the chips.

The other problem with the grocery store? I always run into clients. I'm usually wearing an old pair of jeans or a sweat suit, and I'm lucky if I've combed my hair, and, no, I haven't showered. At first, my clients don't recognize me in my mommy cape. They've never seen me without high heels and lipstick. I politely say hello and offer my hand for a firm handshake. They stare at me, and then at my children. Then it dawns on them, *Lady Lawyer was pregnant all those years. I guess that means she has children of her own.* We usually have a good laugh as I introduce them to Weekend Mommy and make small talk as I chase Abby who is headed back to the soup aisle. I know they are thinking I can't control my own children. They're also looking at all the junk in my cart and thinking I must be a terrible mother. I'm careful to point out that most of the junk is actually for Doug. Sure, I've given in on the Fruit Loops and Cookie Crisp, but there's lots of produce and vegetables buried under the sugar cereal and chips.

I've heard that Internet grocery shopping is quite the rage. I can see the benefits. No screaming kids. No heavy carts. No rushing around on Saturday morning. No surprise purchases. No colored marshmallows or Cookie Crisp. No running into clients that I don't want to see on the weekend. It seems like a no-brainer; I should just do it all online.

Unfortunately, I can't give up the grocery store. I can't explain it. It all stems from my unwillingness to delegate. Besides, online shopping involves the computer. By Saturday morning, I'm tired of sitting in front of a computer, and I'm tired of my kids seeing me sit in front of a computer. Part of me thinks it's good for the kids to join me in the simple task of buying food for the family. Even if it takes us twice as long and I spend twice as much money; it's teamwork.

Adventures at Macy's

Shopping for clothes is another story. As much as I've tried, the kids and I can't achieve teamwork in the department store. When Anna was two, she was running around Macy's while Doug and I were foolish enough to think we could shop. Anna, like most kids, was intrigued by the escalator. I probably should have stopped her, but before I could she managed to figure out how to press the stop button on the escalator and completely terrified some elderly woman who almost wiped out in midstream. Luckily, no one was hurt. We got kicked out of Macy's before we even got a chance to use our coupons, and it took me awhile to get up the nerve to go back. Without Anna.

I still take my kids to department stores, although I'm much more careful around escalators. After the incident with Anna at Macy's, the manager put a warning sign and safety guard on the stop button. It was long overdue. I like to think that Anna actually saved a few lives in the process. And I usually don't take all three of them to the department store at once. Nick really hates to shop for clothes and will wear whatever I buy him, so he usually stays home. Not so with Anna. I've tried to buy her clothes without her. She won't wear them. She has her own style and makes her own fashion choices. Besides, now that she's getting a little older, she has fun shopping with Devoted Mommy. And they don't even recognize her any more at Macy's as the girl who stopped the escalator.

Abby, of course, always wants to tag along with her big sister, so we spend most of our time chasing Abby through the aisles and trying to find her when she hides inside the clothing racks. Department stores are a child's paradise for hide-and-seek. I've come close, but I haven't lost a child yet. Abby hasn't had any incidents with escalators, although she got on an elevator once alone. The door shut before we could stop her, and she ended up in the lingerie department two floors above us. Fortunately, the ladies in lingerie quickly realized Abby was out of place and tracked us down. We didn't even get kicked out of the store. I ended up buying some much-needed bras, and everyone was happy.

But Abby has developed a nasty shoplifting habit, especially with jewelry, and we often have to make unexpected returns. She probably wouldn't shoplift in department stores if I just exerted more control over her in the grocery store. It's all my fault. I should have nipped the soup and raw almonds in the bud. Now, she's moved on to bigger-ticket items. She's too young for me to explain the consequences of prison, so Anna and I have to go back and apologize to the cashier and return the jewelry. It's embarrassing, even for Anna.

When it comes to clothes, I used to be the shopping queen. These days, I rarely have the time or the energy to shop for myself.

Especially the way I like to shop. It's all about the hunt. I'm never too proud to admit that Lady Lawyer finds her best deals at the outlets and the clearance rack. I learned that from my mother. Why pay full price for anything when it will go on sale next week? Unfortunately the hunt takes time, something I don't have to spare. "Sorry, Nick, I can't come to your baseball game this morning because I need to shop the twelve-hour sale, and early bird deals end at noon."

Encouraging Amy shares my passion for bargain shopping and understands my crazy schedule. So she will call me from Vegas when she spots a high-fashion item on the clearance rack. She has the finest taste in the family, and she's learned to shop in style on a pastor's salary. When she calls, I know it must be good, and I write her a check without reservation. Doug is always suspicious and wonders why my sister has to find me clothes across the country, but even he can't argue with her taste. I always get compliments when Encouraging Amy picks out my clothes. Someone will comment, "Wow, I love that unique red suit. Where did you find it?" At this point, I should just smile politely and accept a compliment. But I can't. Instead, I have to tell the whole story—how my sister who lives on a pastor's salary is the best personal shopper around, and she finds bargain basement deals at the outlets in Vegas.

"This suit was regularly listed at $800, but Amy found it on clearance for $59.99 at the Rack." Fellow bargain shoppers appreciate the story.

But others just give me a blank stare, as if to say, "Sorry I asked. You must be really cheap to make your sister shop for you from Vegas. Can't you just shop at the local department store like the rest of us?"

I've tried to shop for myself with the kids. It's just too hard. Nick complains the whole time. Anna just keeps bugging me to go to the girls' department. Abby keeps pulling things off the racks and throws a fit when I don't let her try them on. So I squeeze shopping in when I'm by myself. And I'm known to go without meals on business trips just to have time for the outlets. I can eat at home.

Christmas

Just when I think I have shopping under control, Christmas rolls around the corner. Why can't I just focus on preparing for the birth of Jesus? Every year, I tell myself, *It will be different next year.* Instead I continue to subject myself to a new level of insanity. When you add up immediate family, grandparents, friends, two large extended families of nieces and nephews, teachers, Sunday school helpers, and favorite babysitters, I'm buying Christmas presents for about fifty people. It's unthinkable.

My kids see me running around in circles wrapping presents and making lists, and I have to wonder what kind of message I am sending them. That the greatest event in history is celebrated by buying your friends and family lots of stuff they don't need? That more is better? Or that Devoted Mommy doesn't have time to play for the next two months because she's in charge of Christmas? Buying stuff takes lots of time, not to mention lots of mental energy and focus.

Christmas is the absolute test of my shopping skills, developed only after years of hard training and practice. My favorite time to

Christmas shop is between 9:00 p.m. and midnight. The stores are empty, and Nick loves to tag along. First, we have to put the girls to bed and make sure they are really sleeping. Then we make our list and map out where we need to go first. We sneak out quietly and make a quick stop for coffee. Nick orders a hot chocolate, and I get the usual with a shot of caramel. I'm sick of low carbs, and I really need some sugar to go with the caffeine.

Shopping late with Nick gives us some much-needed time alone to bond. Most weekends, Doug and Nick are inseparable, and I take the girls. Nick and I both miss hanging out, and shopping provides a good excuse. Especially since everyone else is sleeping. Nick always wants to buy Doug something special, which leads us to the dreaded hardware store. I hate shopping for tools. Being around hardware makes me feel like I'm in a foreign country—or worse, completely ill. Last Christmas, Nick was dead set on buying Doug a snow blower. I was thinking about something more inexpensive and practical—like gloves, slippers, or some new underwear. Nick never looks at the price tag and his heart was set, so I broke down and bought the snow blower.

We could barely carry it into the house. We tiptoed inside at 11:00 p.m. and tried to sneak it into the office, quickly wrapping the outside of the box. Doug heard us carrying it in, saw the large, heavy box, and assumed it was a new mower—something he really wanted and needed since the old one died. I didn't have the heart to tell Doug he wasn't going to get his mower for Christmas. At least the snow blower was a complete surprise, and Nick was thrilled. Unfortunately it didn't snow all winter. Nick waited and waited. We'd get an inch or two, and it would melt by morning. By February,

Doug finally gave up and returned the snow blower for a new mower. Nick helped pick out the new mower, and everyone was happy. The next week, we got two feet of snow.

For weeks after Christmas, our house is completely cluttered with stuff. The kids have boxes and boxes of presents, and it's literally shameful. Usually we have a few duplicates—an extra set of Legos, a game we already have in the closet, or two of the same craft project. Do we donate the extra items to children in need? Not exactly. Instead, Nick is usually asking to go shopping again, to exchange all of our extra gifts for more. I try to explain to him that it's wrong to covet, and that you can't take all your stuff with you when you die, just your soul. He still doesn't seem to get it.

More Shoes

I can talk all I want, but I'm not exactly the most compelling role model. Talk is cheap. I need to start simplifying. And soon. Just look at my shoe collection.

The other day I was headed to work, and I couldn't find a suitable pair of shoes. I'm sure it's a sin to own as many shoes as I do, so I've stopped counting. But this particular morning, I couldn't find a single pair to match my outfit. Where were all my shoes? About twenty pairs were missing.

The culprits? Anna and Abby, of course. They had taken my high heels to the playroom to open their own shoe store.

Most kids are having tea parties, playing house, or make-believe shopping at the grocery store. Not my girls. They've set up their own shoe department. For the price of my lunch, I could buy a pair of my own shoes and wear them to work. Not just any pair. If I wanted a pair that matched my outfit, it would cost more. Anna was in full sales mode, trying to show me how each pair was just my size. And Abby kept trying to convince me to wear the leopard-skin shoes with my pink suit, even though I already had a perfect pink pair of shoes to match my outfit. She was already wearing the pink shoes and wanted to keep them at home, to go with her princess dress. I finally prevailed with some good old-fashioned bribery. A time-out just didn't seem to fit the mood. "If you give Mommy the pink shoes, you can wear one of Anna's blue princess dresses and put on matching blue shoes." Anna gave me a frown, but Abby quickly complied, and I could finally get dressed for work.

The shoe store was more than a wake-up call. Nick was already obsessed with having more stuff, Anna would soon follow right behind, and Abby was the only two-year-old I knew with a shoe addiction. If I didn't intervene quickly, my kids would drown in a sea of materialism, maybe forever. Devoted Mommy decided that we should immediately start shopping for needy children.

We set out for the toy store, and the kids each got to pick out their own presents for a child of the same sex and similar age. It's a start, but it's not as if we even put a dent in world poverty. Of course we want to do so much more for the needy, but it's easier said than done when I work all week, live in the most homogenous suburb around, and go out of my way to constantly put my kids in a "safe" environment. When they get a little older, we can go to the soup kitchen or adopt a needy family.

I know I should be doing more to cultivate a spirit of gratitude and service, but right now, I have too many excuses. I simply don't have the time. It's too dangerous to take my kids to *that* side of town. I'm afraid that Abby would make a mess in the soup kitchen or, worse yet, steal the soup. My own family has enough needs right now. We can always just give money. I would just be a Band-Aid to problems that are bigger than I can tackle. It's not like I can make a real commitment. I don't want to be one of those people who says she is going to effect change and then do nothing. Isn't it better not to get involved at all? Maybe when I retire and the kids move out, then I can really focus on helping all those needy families. I'm feeling pretty needy myself these days.

Like most things in life, if I waited for the perfect timing, I would stand by and do nothing. Sure, like most working mothers, I'm pretty overwhelmed, but if I used this excuse every time I saw a need outside of my own family, I would become completely and totally self-absorbed. Even more troubling? My children would become completely self-absorbed. So I have a responsibility not to be satisfied with the status quo and teach them to invest their treasures in things that won't rot, decay, or be destroyed. While I regularly fall far short of this command and probably shop more than I should, I fully intend to keep pressing forward.

In today's culture, it's hard to teach my kids that our lives are about more than our material possessions. After all, having more stuff is cool, isn't it? So we read the story of the rich fool who had such a good crop that he tore down his barns, built bigger barns, and thought he was set for life. The only problem? God said to him, "You fool! This very night your life will be demanded from you. Then who will get what you have prepared for yourself?"[1] Pastor Eric explained that the big barns were not the problem—the problem was the rich fool's heart. In addition to the rich fool being completely selfish and not using his possessions for anyone other than himself, he was placing his security in things that were temporal—things he could never take with him. In simple terms, it was a bad investment.

So while "more stuff" can make us happy for a season, I try to explain to my kids that we really need to invest in things that will last, like other people. And the more I focus on the needs of others and teach my children to do the same, the less we shop and the more we realize just how much we really have.

NINE

Generations of Superwomen

> Two are better than one, because they have a good return for their work.... Though one may be overpowered, two can defend themselves. A cord of three strands is not quickly broken.
>
> Ecclesiastes 4:9, 12

There is a generation of women that I really want my children to know. Many of these women are first-generation Americans. They are tested and strong. They have lost children and hold their heads high in public, even though they may sob in their beds at night. Many of them don't talk about their faith; they just model it. They live modestly, never had their "own" income, and work hard running their homes. They don't complain, because they know life isn't easy. They never expected it to be easy. Unlike my generation, they never thought they could have it all. They never got pedicures or went out for girls' night or expected anything other than hard work and the reward of children and grandchildren who would bless them for years to come. On the outside, these women sometimes appear hard and calloused. (Who could blame them?) But on the inside, they are warm, loving, and generous.

Most of us know a woman who fits this mold—a grandmother, an aunt, or even a neighbor. I was recently talking to one of my colleagues, George the Greek, about this lost generation of women who are sorely missed by their children and grandchildren. Every family has a matriarch. For George, his Yaya (grandmother) was the glue that held the family together. We both agreed that watching *My Big Fat Greek Wedding* was a bonding experience for those of us who grew up around ethnic families. George had fond memories of his Greek Orthodox Easter—roasting a whole lamb with the eyes still in it, in his front yard. His neighbors would drive by and stare, and he would feel sorry for them and think, *They must not have nice families.*

Yaya would shake her head and say, "These people will never know what they are missing. Just make sure you marry a girl who is Greek."

While I was in college, I began to think deeply about my own grandmothers, both who ruled their respective homes with hard work and faith, but little emotion. My paternal grandmother, whom we called "Granny," struck fear in our hearts when she shook that bony German finger, but I was grateful for the special bond we shared right before she passed. I was crushed when she died right before my wedding—just as we were getting closer—and I realized that one day soon, this generation of women would be gone. How could I learn from them?

My maternal grandmother, "Grandma," was still alive. Although we had never been close, I knew I had much to learn from her. So I decided to write a book about Grandma and her remarkable generational values, and I started to take notes in my journal.

Now, when you're getting ready to enter law school and you're newly married, you have better things to do than write a book. About that time Tom Brokaw wrote *The Greatest Generation* and stole my idea. Okay, maybe his book wasn't just about women, but he had made the generational points (much better than I) and had left me with nothing to write about. So I put the journal away and stopped writing. Somehow, I knew I would pull it out again to finish the rest of the story.

Grandma died while I was pregnant with Nick, and it was only after her death that I connected the dots. Why is it that death has a way of bringing greater clarity? It wasn't just that my grandmothers would be missed and learned from; they were still a part of me in many ways. My journey as a working mother had everything to do with the women who came before me, even though they didn't work outside the home. As for Grandma, I can hardly deny that her stubborn spirit and determination formed the core traits of Lady Lawyer, and I'm thankful that her independence and fierce loyalty to family are stamped on my character forever.

I realize my stories about Grandma on the pages to come are unique to my own family and experiences, so please think about your own matriarch—a grandmother, a mother, or an aunt—who has made you the working woman you are today. As the saying goes, blood is thicker than water.

D'Ercole Blood

When Anna is being particularly stubborn, Doug says she has "D'Ercole blood." Rose Catropa D'Ercole, my grandma, had a mind of her own.

I was not her favorite and she never pretended otherwise. Of my sisters, I was the only one who never learned how to sew. It bothered Grandma, and she let me know it. I also hated to clean my room. I never made my bed, and everyone was always picking up after me. Grandma would tell me I was just like her baby sister, Helen. Helen was lazy, and made everyone else do her work. Grandma would call me "Miss Prissy" and say, "The baby in the family is always spoiled." Did I mention that Helen was also the baby?

I liked being spoiled. I also had my mother telling me every day that I was just fine the way I was, so I never took Grandma's comments to heart. Her criticism helped me develop a thick skin—something Lady Lawyer would thank her for years later.

Maybe I couldn't sew, but I could do other things. And I wasn't really interested in sewing anyway. Even at a young age, I could do the math. By the time my sisters found a suitable pattern, bought the material, pinned and cut the material to the pattern, and started sewing, they had already spent more time and money on a dress that probably wouldn't fit. And that doesn't even count the time putting on buttons, zippers, and other finishing touches. Half the time, our old Singer machine would jam, and then they had to rip out the thread by hand and start the whole thing over. No thank you. I had better things to do with my time.

I was more interested in books. And with all that reading, I never had time to clean my room. This is where Grandma came in. She couldn't help herself, and every time she visited, she would unilaterally purge my room of my worn clothes, old toys, or other favorite items she said I was "too big for." How could I stop her? Someone had to clean my room, and I wasn't going to lift a finger. It would happen during her annual summer visit, a visit that would last days or weeks depending on how well she and my father tolerated each other. He was always respectful of Grandma, but he wasn't her favorite either, and she let him know it. Besides, he was used to being in charge. He was the king of the castle, except when Grandma visited. She cooked food he didn't like, watched shows on TV he didn't want to watch, read his paper before he came home from work, and even took over his chair. It wasn't intentional, it was just her nature. She didn't know how to be anything but in charge.

My sisters and I got a kick out of seeing her dethrone the king, something my mother wouldn't dream of. By the end of her visit, she would buy him a case of beer, and they would part on good terms. Grandma couldn't drive, so she would ask my mother to take her to the grocery store. They would always get separate carts, and my mother would shudder every time we hit the beer aisle and say, "He doesn't need it, Mum." Grandma would ignore her objections every time and say under her breath, "It won't hurt him, Stella." It was her way of making peace with him, something he always appreciated.

After we secured the beer, Grandma would move on to the other items on her list, including olive oil, peppers, sausage, and meat for her sauce. She would tell me I could have anything I wanted, and I would always pick out a bag of puffed cheese curls—the kind that melt in your mouth and make your hands orange from all the food coloring. We'd have a few duplicates with my mother at the checkout, so Grandma would push ahead and make sure she got in line before my mother, pulling crisp bills out of her pocketbook (she never owned a credit card) and elbowing my mother who always tried to pay first. She and my mother would argue, and my mother would insist on paying for everything but the beer.

Ethnic women can be extremely loud at the grocery store, especially when they're fighting, and everyone would stare. Grandma was so loud that even my mother relented and let her pay for her own groceries. Sometimes sheer volume can win an argument, especially in public. I can't help thinking the stares prepared me for Devoted Mommy's shopping adventures.

Men, Mosquitoes, and Meatballs

The only time Grandma rested was in the evenings on the back porch. As much as she loved the summer air, she would constantly complain about the mosquitoes that always plagued our Ohio summers. "Your Aunt Rose doesn't get these mosquitoes in California," she would say. I would put on shows for Grandma with dancing and singing, and she would clap and tell me stories about my grandfather "Papa" and growing up in West Aliquippa, Pennsylvania. She loved to tell stories about all the famous people that grew up in West Aliquippa, like the composer Henry Mancini. My uncle Anthony would make fun of Henry and call him a sissy for practicing the piano and being a mama's boy instead of playing baseball with the neighborhood. Uncle Anthony played ball with the Yankees farm team and Mickey

Mantle until the bottle got the best of him. Grandma would get a sad look in her eye, and I knew not to ask questions.

Grandma's strength always drew in neighborhood women, and she would update our family on the local gossip as our next-door neighbor, the only divorced woman around, would visit every evening. We would learn who was cheating, who was dating, and who was divorcing. This was a far cry from my mother, who never entertained gossip or attempted to meddle in anyone's business. A cheating man was a no-good man. There were no shades of gray when it came to fidelity and commitment. Men who cheated would burn in hell. And she didn't feel sorry for them.

When Blonde Sister began to date the man who would become her husband, Grandma first asked about his nationality: "What is he?" Blonde Sister jokingly told Grandma that he was half "hillbilly." This was a serious mistake. Grandma had lived near a group of hillbillies in West Aliquippa, and she proclaimed that they were the dirtiest people on the face of the earth. The other strike against him? He was a football player. Never mind that his football scholarship gave him a full ride to college, where he worked hard inside and outside the classroom, earning straight As. All football players were dumb, not to mention self-centered. We laugh about it today, but poor Blonde Sister shed her share of tears for dating and then marrying a "hillbilly football player." Did I mention that he isn't even a hillbilly?

Sometimes you just can't change a woman's mind. No matter how hard you try, it's useless. Strong, obstreperous women tend to repel some people. Not me. Instead, I am drawn to them. Doug always tells me I have managed to pick the most overbearing friends, starting with Sassy Shelly, the only woman in the world Doug refuses to argue with. Why? It's completely useless. No one has ever won an argument with her. There are two ways to see the world: her way or no way. And Jock Jill is the last person you want to meet in the courtroom. She'll eat you alive, and most people, except me, are afraid to ruffle her feathers. But I find her rougher edges endearing. I am right at home with hardheaded women.

The D'Ercole women share this trait, and my father likes to proclaim that we are the most stubborn women on the face of the earth. I used to think he was overreaching. Then I had Anna and Abby. Just try talking Anna out of wearing leopard tank top on a cold winter morning.

Stubborn as she was, Grandma, like most of her generation, wasn't afraid of a day's work. While we spent our evenings on the back porch, the days were full of labor. Scrubbing, mopping, sweeping, dusting, washing, ironing, and drying. Grandma was very passionate about her work. She would wash windows and walls, and even though she was only five feet tall and aging, she would stand on a ladder just to dust the light fixtures or reach for the corner cobwebs with her broom. A dirty house was something to be ashamed of, and a clean house was a woman's crown.

The best part of the day was spent in the sanctuary of the kitchen, the hottest room in the house in the summer heat. Hot enough to keep the men out, but not hot enough to keep three generations of women from gathering, even without air conditioning. It doesn't matter if you have an empty dining room, comfortable furniture, or a cozy great room with plenty of seating. Women will gather in the kitchen—no matter the size or the available seating.

The reason? We know where the action is. Kitchen conversation is sacred. It was in the kitchen that Grandma told us the story of how she married Papa not knowing his true age. He lied to her before the wedding, and it wasn't until after they were married that she learned he was sixteen years her senior. Fortunately, her fierce independence enabled her to care for herself on a small pension after his death. She never bought anything for herself and always showered her grandchildren with cash. For an eighth-grade education, she knew more about politics than both of my parents combined. She devoured the newspaper every day and never missed a current event.

But even more than politics, Grandma's favorite subject of kitchen conversation was my mother. Like a proud mother, she loved to brag about her own daughter in front of her, as if she wasn't in the room. As harsh as Grandma was with the rest of the world, I never heard her give anything but praise for my mother. "Saint Stella," Grandma would call her. She loved to tell us stories about how my mother would gladly iron the family shirts, would never complain about housework, and most importantly, how she had her choice of boyfriends. In fact, she was the envy of every young woman in Aliquippa, officially nominated as the "Woof Girl" of Aliquippa High. My mother had smart boyfriends, rich boyfriends, and—most importantly—Italian boyfriends.

Not being Italian was my father's first mistake. But his fatal mistake was much more serious. He didn't like Grandma's cooking, and he didn't even fake it. Grandma would spend hours laboring over the very foods he didn't like—ravioli, gnocchi, minestrone, wedding soup, and pizzelles. Not only did he not like these foods, he complained when they were served, so much that my mother had to make him his own plate of plain spaghetti, the only pasta he would eat. My father would be served first. Never mind whether or not he liked the food. I always liked Grandma's meatballs better than my mother's, although I would never admit it. But I had to agree with my father about the sauce. I was used to my mother's sauce. Grandma always made her sauce by first browning a roast, and she usually left the fat in for flavor. Too much fat for me. Yet another thing for my father to complain about.

Sometimes, I wished he would just keep his mouth shut and eat, but like Grandma, keeping quiet wasn't his nature. Not to mention that he liked to tease Grandma, and the more he got a reaction out of her, the more it entertained him. Grandma would yell at him and tell him how lucky he was to have my mother. Then she would proclaim, "Uncle Sam will eat anything that Aunt Rose puts in front of him." She would always end the sentence by saying, "He will even eat dog food."

At least she never talked about my father behind his back. One thing I fully appreciate about Grandma's generation of women is their honesty. Brutal honesty. Even Lady Lawyer doesn't have the guts to tell people what she really thinks, so she acts diplomatic on the outside so later on she can undermine them when they're not around to defend themselves. Not Grandma. If she had something to say, she'd say it right to your face. When I was dating Doug, he was standing right next to me in the kitchen when Grandma proclaimed that I was spending too much time with "that boy." She never called him by name until long after we were married.

Communal Living

Grandma modeled community—a real sense of knowing and caring for your neighbors—so much that often I long for a houseful of women making pasta together or sitting on my back porch. Most of us live far away from family, don't know our neighbors, and certainly don't hang out on our back porches for conversation when we can be talking on our cell phones or multitasking on our laptops. Yet my roots convince me that women were designed to live together in large communities. Unfortunately Doug has informed me he has no interest in communal living. So I hold tightly to the memories of my mother's kitchen, and I live for my college reunions every few years.

The last college reunion was at my house. We don't get hotel rooms. It's against the rules. Husbands are invited but not expected to attend, and children are always welcome. So last year we had a houseful of eight women, one brave husband (not counting mine), and a dozen children under the age of five. Doug made it until Sunday afternoon; then he locked himself in our bedroom until everyone left Monday evening. Built Becky had taken all the furniture out of my living room and turned it into a fitness studio, and Self-Employed Stefanie and Trusting Tracy had turned my kitchen upside down entertaining guests while Meticulous Molly and Caring Christie cleaned up everyone's messes. It was just like we were back in college. At least I got communal living out of my system for a few years.

Sometimes I still wonder, didn't Grandma have it right? Why are most women trying to do it all alone? In the New Testament church the believers were devoted "to the apostles' teaching and to the fellowship, to the breaking of bread and to prayer."[1] This requires a devotion to *other people.* But in today's modern church, it's unusual for families to live together in rich community. In fact, I would venture to guess that in circumstances when the mother works outside the home, the family is less likely to be involved in a church. Why? Probably a variety of reasons. Like me, some working mothers have felt judged by the church so they've decided to pull away. Others are simply too busy, too overwhelmed, or don't feel like the church can even begin to relate to their daily world. The result? Too many of us feel as if we are all alone. Why can't we live in a greater sense of community with other mothers and families? After all, wouldn't communal living be ideal for the working mother? Is a sense of community completely lost in my generation?

I was recently talking with my brother-in-law Jon (Encouraging Amy's husband) about their church in Las Vegas where he serves as one of the pastors. No, it's not perfect—there's no such thing as a perfect church—but they really take the message of community to heart. So, you don't have to clean up your act and become the "church lady" before you'll be accepted. Instead, they preach the three Bs—belong, believe, and *then* behave. There's something about belonging first that really has a nice ring. It's all about being part of a community—knowing that you have a "neighborhood" to call home. Too many of us are sitting at home and talking on our cell phones or glued to the TV watching chick flicks when what we really need is a live group of women to talk with, laugh with, and even cry with—like the women who gathered around my mother's kitchen when Grandma visited.

Lots of working mothers just need to hear that they belong.

Saying Goodbye

The hard thing about losing people you love is you're never ready to say goodbye. And looking back at those last few years, I could have learned so much more from Grandma. But I was busy getting ready to be Lady Lawyer, and I rarely saw Grandma after I went to law school. She traveled less in her late years, and it was always inconvenient for me to visit her. She continued to play favorites. I visited her during my second year of law school with Artist Sister, who was then in graduate school. She gave Artist Sister a twenty-dollar bill right in front of me and wished her luck in school. She turned to me and said, "Tell Doug I said hello." Grandma eventually learned to like Doug. In addition to being Italian, he scrubbed her favorite pan, ate her food, and even sat in the kitchen and listened to her stories. But Artist Sister was by far her favorite, and Grandma always felt sorry for her because she didn't marry until she was almost forty. "Poor Marybeth. She still isn't married," Grandma would say. And Grandma would always say that she hoped and prayed Marybeth would get married before it was "too late." Of course, we all knew what that meant. Soon, Artist Sister would be too old to bear children, and a husband was a necessary part of the progression to motherhood.

Grandma understood, as I do now, the wonderful gift of motherhood. But she never got to see me wear my mommy cape. I was four months pregnant with Nick at her funeral. The last thing she told me was that I was going to have a boy, something she rarely got wrong. Like so many women who never had ultrasounds or genetic testing to determine gender, she could just look at a pregnant woman (Is she carrying "low" or "wide"?) and know the sex of the child immediately.

I know we would have finally bonded after I became a mother. Sure, she probably would have given me her share of criticism, but I would gladly take it to have her back. I can hear her saying, "Miss Prissy is always off traveling while Doug takes care of those poor kids at home. And did you hear about that nanny who fell asleep in the attic?" But she would understand my deep love for my children and would feed them in my mother's kitchen, telling the same stories over and over again. In the end they all would love her, and she would teach them the importance of family values and community.

When Doug says that the girls and I have D'Ercole blood, we take it as a compliment. I pray that my girls will have Grandma's determination, independence, and zeal for life. Grandma had all the traits to be a great lawyer in her time—articulate, clever, and tenacious. She could have held her own with Sassy Shelly and even rivaled Jock Jill in the courtroom. I'm just thankful she made an even better grandmother and mother.

So many of the women who came before us would have been successful career women in their time. Like Grandma, they were working mothers in every sense of the word. They modeled their faith by putting their families first and, unlike us, they didn't complain about having more time for themselves or needing their own "space." They were proud to be mothers first and modeled rich community. We have so much to learn from their generation of Superwomen.

TEN

The Bread of Life

> Do not work for food that spoils, but for food that endures to eternal life....
>
> I am the bread of life. He who comes to me will never go hungry, and he who believes in me will never be thirsty.
>
> John 6:27, 35

Unlike Grandma, I will never be a domestic goddess. I hate to clean. I can't even tell you the last time I pulled out an iron. I'm terribly disorganized and can barely keep up with the kids' schedules, let alone my personal mail. And I hate to decorate. The last time we got a new couch, Abby had Vaseline smeared all over it within an hour of delivery (and, no, we didn't buy the fabric protection plan). Maybe I'll decorate when the kids get older. For now, why waste the creative energy, time, and money?

I may not clean, sew, organize, or decorate. But my roots have taught me the central importance of food in my family life. How could I ever live with myself if I relinquished the fundamental God-given right of preparing daily bread for my family? The women in my family were largely judged on the food they put on the table. Why should I be any different?

My First Apron

It's not like I set out to cook. Like everything else on my journey, it just sort of happened.

After I entered law school, Doug and I were completely broke. We quickly found that if we shopped smart and were a little creative, we could get by eating well on a shoestring budget. Pasta, our all-time staple, was cheap. And my mother provided me with an endless supply of homemade tomato sauce through law school. I know what you're thinking: Why couldn't a grown woman scrape a few bucks together and buy her own sauce at the grocery? It's simple. I'm spoiled. No canned or bottled sauce tastes as good as my mother's.

Not being able to eat anyone else's sauce had its consequences, especially when my mother lived two hours away. And our first apartment barely had enough room in the freezer for the ice trays, let alone containers of frozen sauce. The solution? I just had to learn how to make it myself. I've always been practical about domestic work, and I could see that cooking—unlike cleaning the toilet or dusting cobwebs—had some immediate and tangible benefits. Like feeding us. So my mother bought me one of those sixteen-quart stockpots, and I never looked back.

Kids in the Kitchen

Nick's favorite food is spaghetti, and he also refuses to eat store-bought sauce. I can't blame him. I've created a monster. If you open my freezer, it's packed with frozen sauce. I have it down to a science. Now that I have a commercial stovetop with six burners, I've upgraded to the twenty-quart pot. It still takes a full day to make a pot of sauce, and if I'm quick enough I get started early in the morning before my helpers get out of bed.

My kids all love to cook. Anna is in charge of stirring, Nick is in charge of rolling the meatballs, and we're all in charge of cleaning up Abby's messes. Maybe we should try to stop her from helping, but I don't believe in crushing the spirit of a two-year-old, even if it does take twice as long to accomplish a simple task. Besides, I'm not in a hurry. Cooking together beats just about any other family activity, and Abby is quickly learning to embrace her roots.

Besides sauce, our favorite projects include homemade pasta and variety of soups, birthday cakes, and all types of cookies. Every holiday we make cutout cookies, even though I hate cleaning up the mess. The kids end up eating half the dough, and Abby usually has about an inch of flour on the floor. She eats icing by the spoonfuls, and I always regret it when it's 10:00 p.m., and I'm exhausted and she's still bouncing off the walls.

The kids decorate the cookies in a variety of colors, and we're each careful to respect everyone else's work and talent. No one will eat Abby's cookies because she licks all the icing before, during, and after she finishes her work. I've become completely obsessive about decorating "my" cookies ever since Nick bought me my first cake-decorating set. The Christmas trees have to be green with white glitter for snowflakes and red bulbs. And the Easter eggs are always purple and yellow, with alternating stripes. I love saving them for my mother so she can marvel about them for weeks. "How do you ever find the time, Susan?"

There is nothing more rewarding than sitting down to a meal with your children, especially when they've helped prepare the food. Sunday afternoon dinners are sacred and easily my favorite time of the week. Give me a kitchen full of hungry kids, a glass of red wine, and an apron and I'm happy as a clam. No TV, no distractions, no rushing around, and no billable hours. We just sit and eat, and there's always plenty of food. It's one thing to spend family time together. Sharing a meal is intimate.

Once again, Lady Lawyer and Devoted Mommy have something in common. They're both food snobs. Lady Lawyer prefers to dine at the finest restaurants, especially when she's entertaining her clients. And Devoted Mommy is completely tired of her kids eating junk under everyone else's watch, so she always refuses the kids' repeated requests for fast food. Whenever we eat out, I'm always scrutinizing the food, thinking about how I could have made it better at home. Most restaurants are overrated and overpriced, and the kids always order the same greasy foods. Their eyes are usually bigger than their stomachs, and we always order too much. We take the extras home with good intentions, but inevitably leftovers end up in the trash. Who wants to eat a greasy, soggy kid's meal the next day?

Even Doug prefers to eat at home. We have always shared a special bond over food. Like me, he appreciates both the quality and experience of a good meal, something not easily accomplished in kid-friendly restaurants. Even if the food is good, we usually end up chasing Abby around because she won't sit in her seat, and as soon as we get our food, we wolf it down in about five minutes because we know our time is limited before someone is going to ask us to leave. It's no way to enjoy a meal.

This is why whenever Doug and I get out for dinner alone, we try to pick a restaurant that doesn't accommodate children. Sometimes, some inexperienced parents will bring their toddler along, and I join in with the rest of the crowd and give dirty looks. Who wants to be around screaming kids when you just left yours at home? It's one thing to have your own children ruin a meal. But somebody else's kids? I'd rather stay at home.

Unfortunately, eating at home isn't always that simple. Someone has to cook. Doug will grill hamburgers, boil rice, or stick a casserole in the oven. And he makes and rolls the dough for homemade ravioli every Christmas Eve. But most of the other daily meals in our house fall squarely on my shoulders. If I don't plan it, it doesn't get done. So my Sunday afternoons are usually spent planning dinners for the week. While I've got a roast in the oven, there's soup cooking on the stove, and a whole chicken in the crock pot that I'm going to debone later for casseroles and quesadillas. The kitchen is about 105 degrees, and at the end of the day Devoted Mommy is tired but strangely satisfied. At least we will have dinners through Wednesday. Then it's back to pasta and frozen dinners.

My Little Secret

Most people are shocked to hear that Lady Lawyer spends her Sundays cooking. Like my parents. They didn't think I could boil water for the first ten years I was married. My mother just assumed Doug did all the cooking, and would ask him questions such as how he makes his sauce and what brand of olive oil he prefers. He would play along with it, and it would make me furious. No one believed that I could cook.

However, there are certain advantages to having your family think you can't cook. Advantage number one: You don't have to bring side dishes and casseroles to family cookouts. I have a special exemption. My sisters all say, "Susie is just too busy to cook," and my mother insists, "Please don't bring anything. We already have too much food." It's hard to argue with that rationale. So just like Aunt Helen, I usually sit back and let everyone else do my work.

So long as my secret is safe, I still don't have to lift a finger. Everyone thinks I'm too busy. But sometimes I get a new recipe that I can't help sharing with my sisters. There's nothing like having everyone enjoy your creations or hearing, "Wow! That's the best avocado dip I've ever tasted." So, a few times a year, I actually contribute something to the meal.

When my mother visits, she likes to do all the cooking. It's in her blood, just like it was in Grandma's. Some women just can't enter a home without taking over. She brings her own supplies, despite my insistence that I have spices and regular baking staples in my kitchen. Even though I generally welcome domestic takeovers, I finally couldn't hold back anymore. I really wanted to show her I could cook. So I insisted on preparing the meal. She wouldn't hear of it at first, but after some arm twisting, she finally gave in. I told her that I really wanted her to spend quality time with my kids since they absolutely adore her and see her once a month if we're lucky. Why spend your time in front of the stove when three children are all begging for your attention? She couldn't disagree, so I made her pork tenderloin with stir-fried vegetables and garlic smashed potatoes. She was in heaven. She talked about my pork tenderloin for weeks, and even my sisters were a little annoyed that I had become Julia Child overnight. Never mind that they had been bringing casseroles, dips, and main courses to family functions for years. I was now the most recognized chef in the family. It would cost me the exemption, but it was well worth it.

If only Grandma could see me now.

Leftovers and Junk Food

When guests enter your home, the first thing to do is offer them something to eat. I learned this from my mother. Inexperienced guests at her home smile and politely refuse. This is their first mistake. She won't take no for an answer and will even take personal offense. "What's the matter, don't you like pie?" The more you refuse, the more she will insist, and if you claim you are full she will pack it up and make you take it with you. She makes the best pies around, and—unlike her sauce—I won't even attempt to replicate them. I'm too afraid of failure when the standards are this high. After eating some pie, she'll entice you with brownies, chocolates, or some homemade cookies. Who couldn't feel at home?

Guests are also good at getting rid of leftovers. I grew up on leftovers, and as much as we all liked to eat, we weren't allowed to waste. So we would have a meal that included a piece of roast, a pile of dried-out spaghetti, and some leftover casserole. My father would complain like mad, but even he didn't believe in wasting food, and he didn't lift a finger in the kitchen. So, like the rest of us, he ate it.

I try to make my kids clean their plates. I tell them stories about the starving children, and how I always had to clean my plate as a little girl. We have contests. Threats of no dessert or no snacks before bed. But they don't have an appreciation for the evils of wasting food. Part of the problem? They've never seen leftovers for dinner. Doug refuses to eat leftovers, which is where our neighbor Ed the Eater comes in. We can always count on Ed the Eater to clean up anything, which makes me happy because I hate to waste and, like my mother, I love to feed guests. It also takes that extra pressure off the kids, not to mention the guilt off of Devoted Mommy for wasting perfectly good food.

I don't know what upsets me more, wasting food or junk food. Few things irritate me more than my children eating unhealthy snacks. I recently saw some study that working moms are more likely to have overweight children who develop health problems because of all the poor food choices they make when Mom isn't around. Of course, I felt guilty. Just what I needed. Another negative study about working moms. My kids are living proof that validates the study one hundred percent. They love junk.

Even though I wholly embrace healthy eating, I simply don't have time to make them healthy food like they deserve. When it comes to snacks, I'm a terrible packer. Most mothers who have nutritional control over their children carry around these coolers filled with fresh fruits, raw vegetables, and purified water. Not me. It's downright embarrassing when Abby constantly bums food off the other mothers at Nick's baseball games. We usually race to the ball fields right after I get home from work and the poor thing is starving. The other mothers look at me like, "Don't you have your own cooler?" Actually, I don't. I'm lucky if I have an extra diaper on hand, let alone food or water. The few times I actually have snacks on hand, it's because Doug had the foresight to pack. He picks up all the prepackaged garbage at the grocery, but I can't complain because at least he took the initiative, and it stops Abby from eating other people's food.

As much as he tries, Doug has yet to embrace my nutritional standards. He makes up for it in other ways, so I try to turn my head when he feeds the kids junk on a constant basis. For the record, Ho Hos are deadly and even though Doug allows them, I wouldn't feed them to my children if they were the last piece of garbage on the planet.

Why do I spend an inordinate amount of mental energy, time, and passion on food? Maybe I'm trying to overcompensate—the Superwoman complex again—since I'm not domestic in other areas. Maybe I'm just obsessed with food because of my upbringing. Some roots run too deep.

Food for the Soul

As soon as I have some extra time on my hands, I'm going to go through the entire Bible and mark every reference to food. I'll start with Jacob's birthright meal, manna from heaven, Elijah and the ravens, the widow's jar that wouldn't run empty, David and his men eating the consecrated bread, and Daniel's kosher diet plan. I'll then move on to the New Testament, including turning the water into wine, feeding the five thousand, and Jesus' final meal with His friends—the Last Supper. I love to picture Jesus and His disciples in the upper room, reclining at the table. They had shared many meals together before, but when He broke the bread everyone had to know that this one was different. Sometimes I wonder if there will be food in heaven. I'm convinced it would only be the finest of quality, all perfectly made from scratch and no fast food or greasy kids' meals. I get hungry just thinking about it.

As much as I feed and nourish my body, you would think I'd take better care of my soul. Like the body, the soul needs water and food to survive. I've been living on a soul diet of bread and water way too long. In a twisted way, I have bought into the lie that God wants to deprive me with leftovers when He really wants to give me a feast. "No thanks, God, the beef tenderloin and fresh vegetables look wonderful, but I'd really prefer some old, stale bread and trans fats loaded with nitrates." So I miss out on the main course and settle for the very things I don't give my children—leftovers and junk. But God still wants to give me the very best, and He waits patiently until I realize it's right on my plate for the taking.

It reminds me of my Sunday dinners. If I don't want fast food or frozen pizza I have to invest the time and energy in preparing a quality meal. Someone has to do the planning, shopping, cooking, and cleanup for all of us to enjoy a family meal. And as much as I enjoy the food, I really enjoy the experience of spending time together with people I love. If I made the dinner for myself, ate alone, and everyone else just heated up the leftovers, it wouldn't be nearly as enjoyable or rewarding.

Like my Sunday dinners, spiritual food takes time, discipline, and a willing heart. I need to plan in advance, try a few new recipes and patiently wait, being careful not to burn the main course or miss dessert. Sometimes, I wish God would just invent some spiritual fast food for working mothers. Don't we have enough on our plates? How about a pill for complete and total spiritual nutrition? But like my Sunday dinners, I don't think a pill could ever substitute for the experience or relationships involved in the meal.

I still don't have the perfect recipe for spiritual nutrition, and maybe I'll never completely figure it out. But I know that I don't need a pill, I need a Person. Why settle for bread when you can have the Bread of Life?

ELEVEN

When Will I Get Some Rest, God?

> Come to me, all you who are weary and burdened, and I will give you rest.
>
> Matthew 11:28

I am always exhausted. I can't remember the last time I got a good night's sleep. Someone is always up.

My kids have never been good sleepers, starting with Nick. Like most new moms, I was desperate for a formula. So I read all the books that guaranteed he would sleep through the night if I just followed a set of simple instructions. It sounded easy. First, I tried putting him on a rigid feeding schedule. The theory? Demand feeding is evil. As important, no napping during scheduled feedings, and no snacking in between feedings. If he wakes up in the middle of the night, just let him cry it out, and by eight weeks, everyone will be sleeping through the night.

It didn't work. Try keeping a nursing baby awake when he is exhausted. And why would anyone in her right mind wake a baby for a feeding? Everyone knows the old saying, "Don't wake a sleeping baby." So, I moved on to Plan B: the sleep schedule.

Plan B says it's okay to demand feed, but make sure you keep the sleep schedule consistent. Bedtime is always at the same time every night, and naps occur on the appointed hour like clockwork. This worked for a while, so long as the whole family revolved around the "schedule." But some nights Nick would still wake up. I would feed him, and he wouldn't go back to sleep.

Night Wakings

Like most first-time mothers I know, I wasn't very good at letting Nick cry it out. Who wants to let your child cry it out all night when you've barely seen him all day? I tried buying earplugs, but I would still hear him. After about twenty minutes, I would usually give up and go get him. I wanted to hold him, and it was just easier to give in. I would be so exhausted the next morning from letting him "cry it out" that I could barely stay awake at my desk.

Even when Nick would sleep through the night, I would still wake up. It was automatic. I would wake up for feedings, even when he wasn't hungry or awake. Try telling your body clock to reset after months and months of waking in the middle of the night. Like everything else, it takes time. When he finally slept through the night for about a week and my body was finally getting used to the rest, he would get a severe cold and the whole cycle would start over. Again. Everyone knows sick babies don't sleep though the night.

Part of the problem with Nick? He just needs less sleep than the average person—something I didn't realize until years later. Nick and I like to joke about the fact that the two of us are always the last ones up. Like me, he can't turn off his brain, so he always has trouble falling asleep.

As I'm writing and the rest of the house is sleeping, he quietly sneaks in and sits next to me. I can't yell at him; he truly can't fall asleep. So I put my arm around him as he leans over my laptop to see what I'm writing. He keeps asking me when I'm going to write about him getting his tonsils out, and I explain that I am trying to work it in. Then he starts explaining to me how Velcro is made. The guy who invented it was walking his dog when some burr stuck to the dog. This gave him an idea to invent Velcro. The sticky side of Velcro is really small hooks. Nick learned all of this in "Mad Science" class.

I am completely exhausted, but I try to listen. I know firsthand how rough it is when you can't sleep. I turn off my laptop, walk him back to bed, and lie down with him while we talk about who he played with at recess, who's the best tetherball player in the first grade, and what he watched on TV after school—after he did his homework, of course. I tried to get all of this information out of him at the dinner table without success. But something about the evening hour changes all that. He's relaxed and he wants to talk, so I listen. Part of me wants to stay and talk with him, but I know we both need some rest.

Anna needs her beauty rest. She lives life to the fullest, and by the end of the day, she is exhausted. She rarely fights going to bed, but through her toddler years she would wake in the middle of the night for a variety of reasons. She had to go potty. She was too hot. She was too cold. She needed water. She was scared. She couldn't find her blanket. The possibilities were endless. I took her in to her four-year pediatrician's appointment, completely delirious. The pediatrician told me I needed to find Anna some self-soothing techniques: "Tell her she can listen to music in the middle of the night, or better yet, make a tape of Mommy's voice that she can play, telling her not to be afraid." Self-soothing didn't work. Everyone told me to let her cry it out. Easier said than done when you have two other kids who need uninterrupted sleep.

If you're reading this book I probably sound like a complete idiot. Why let a four-year-old push you around and deprive you of sleep? It's a good question for which I have no answer. But time heals all wounds, and shortly after that fourth birthday she outgrew her middle-of-the-night drama, and we all started sleeping again. Just in time for Abby's ear infections to start.

By the time Abby arrived, I was a master at tough love. I let her cry it out early, and she slept through the night almost immediately. I had finally figured it out. Or had I? Try letting a child with a painful ear infection "cry it out" when you haven't seen her all day. The drainage would cause so much pain from lying in her crib, and she would wake up as soon as the Motrin wore off, screaming bloody murder. I'd try to wait until she fell back asleep and prop a pillow underneath her head, but she'd always roll off the pillow. Sometimes it was just easier to hold her in the rocking chair as she slept.

For better or worse, Abby is the Energizer Bunny. The chick never stops. Shortly after she turned two and the ear infections wore off, she started to give up her nap. She would talk and play in her crib for several hours at naptime. Sometimes she would doze off, but then she would be up till midnight. Please don't tell me that 99.9 percent of all the two-year-olds in the world still need a nap. Abby is not one of them. By the end of the day we are completely and totally exhausted. Except Abby.

Some days, I am actually so tired that I can't sleep. It's like having a piece of chocolate cake dangling in front of you and then snatched away. You want to eat it, and you are so close that you can taste it, but it's gone. Most of my friends with young children can relate. Sassy Shelly ended up hiring a sitter in the middle of the night when she had the twins; Jock Jill has a colicky newborn who hasn't slept more than three hours straight since he was born; and Self-Employed Stefanie and I talk about meeting at a midpoint city and renting a hotel room together, just so we can sleep. We know we wouldn't sleep and instead we'd end up staying up all night talking, and we'd be just as tired when we got home. But it's a nice thought.

As much as I travel, you would think I would welcome a night alone in a hotel. Not so. I hate sleeping alone in hotels. Something about it creeps me out. I can't stop thinking about all the germs on the mattress, the strange person who's probably in the connecting room next to me, the filth on the carpet, or the weird security guys who all have access to my room. So I usually don't sleep a wink, and I return home even more exhausted than before I left.

What's even more irritating than not getting any sleep? Doug can sleep through anything. After years of harboring bitterness and resentment, I've just learned to accept it. From what my sisters and girlfriends tell me, this is a genetic disorder in most men. They've simply lost all hearing in the middle of the night. This disorder mysteriously appears in fathers with young children and is possibly irreversible. At least I can channel my anger other places, like the office.

Staying Awake and Faking It

Lady Lawyer can't afford to be exhausted. After about three nights without sleep, I start to become unglued at work. First I get cranky, and then I get downright mean. My body aches as I sit at my desk and I want to cry, but I can't because my day is packed with meetings and conference calls. I lose patience with Crazy Client, I put up more of a fight than usual with Jerk Lawyer, and I can't even bring myself to put on a happy face for the law students. Sometimes I put my head down on my desk, and I'm tempted to just lie on the floor or order one of those long sofas for my office. I could make the room if I just got rid of a few files. My managing partner stops by and says, "Are you okay? You look a little tired."

I respond, "I'm fine, thanks." Rule number one: Don't let people at the office know your home life has completely sucked the life out of you. It's one thing to be a little tired, but no one wants to hire a crazy, delirious lawyer who can't think clearly or walk in a straight line. Working mothers have to stay awake, or at least fake it.

My niece Level-Headed Laura recently asked me, "How am I going to get Harrison to sleep through the night before I go back to work?" My answer: Try anything and everything. Let him cry it out (if you can stand it), use a noise machine or electric fan, put him on a rigid feeding schedule, keep him up all day, and pump him with cereal before bed. So what if the pediatrician says to hold off on solid foods. Your own sanity is at stake, and you can't be a good mother, or a good teacher, if you can't stay awake. Don't forget to pray, and if all else fails, there's always caffeine.

This is where coffee comes in. I am completely and positively addicted to coffee. And I'm not going to even apologize or make excuses. It's my only real vice, besides red wine and chocolate.

The good news? I'm not alone. The rest of America is right there with me. I look around, and there are long lines in the coffee shop. There's nothing like my double-tall, nonfat latte to pull me out of my perpetual state of exhaustion. Before my first sip, I can already feel the buzz. If you haven't noticed, the employees at the coffee shop appear to be some of the happiest people around. The reason? They're not tired. They have an endless supply of caffeine. And as long as I have my caffeine, I can continue to fake it at work and act as if Lady Lawyer really has her act together, even when she is exhausted.

But just when I thought it couldn't get any worse, I reached a new level of sleep deprivation. All five of us had the stomach flu at the same time, and I couldn't keep the usual amount of coffee down to keep myself functioning. Who got up with the kids all hours of the night, repeatedly washing clothes, sheets, and blankets while holding Abby and soothing Nick and Anna because they were all so miserable? You guessed it: me.

Even the flu won't deprive Doug of uninterrupted sleep.

Why do I let him get away with it? Why don't I just wake him and force him to help me in the middle of the night? Been there. Done that. First of all, the kids don't want him. He's not empathetic, and they end up yelling for me. I lie awake listening to him trying to put them back to sleep while they cry, "Where's Mom?" The other problem? He doesn't know how to clean up vomit. Usually he just throws a towel over it and I end up cleaning it the next day, after it's soaked into the carpet. And he always throws the soiled sheets in the washing machine without rinsing them out first. The last time he cleaned up vomit, it took a week for our washing machine to recover. The odor in Abby's room was so heavy that we had to move her out of her room until a professional cleaning company came to clean, disinfect, deodorize, and neutralize. I've since learned that this is another irreversible disorder of fathers with young children. Most of them are simply not wired to clean up vomit.

So when my entire family, including me, came down with the flu, Doug was no help. This is where my mother comes in. She dropped everything and came to town to take care of us. As soon as she arrived, I made Doug take me to the urgent care. Never mind that there is no cure for the flu. I couldn't stop shaking, and I was convinced I was dying. The doctor took one look at me and prescribed a heavy narcotic. He apparently thought I was a drug addict going through withdrawal. He was partially right. I hadn't had caffeine in over four days, and it showed.

I often ask God, *When am I going to get some sleep?* What does God have against sleep anyway? Just because He doesn't sleep, does that mean the rest of us need to go without it? According to the Psalms, He grants sleep to those He loves. Doesn't God love me enough to give me some sleep? It's been about seven years since I've had a good night's rest, and I'd really appreciate it if God would just sprinkle some magic dust my way, just for one night. Sassy Shelly tells me I should just take a sleeping pill, and like Doug I'll never even hear the kids in the middle of the night. But I can't bring myself to do it. It's bad enough being addicted to caffeine; the last thing I want is to get addicted to sleeping medication. What if there was a fire in the middle of the night or a stranger broke in? I might not wake up to rescue my children, and Doug will never hear them.

Maybe sleep is overrated. God doesn't seem to value sleep nearly as much as I do. In fact, bad things always seem to happen when people are sleeping. Samson is sleeping when Delilah cuts his hair. Gideon defeats the enemy camp while they are asleep. The ten virgins are sleeping when the bridegroom arrives. The disciples fall asleep in the garden of Gethsemane when Jesus needs them to watch and pray. Maybe it's not such a bad thing that I'm lacking sleep.

Vacation

What could be more exhausting than working all day, being up all night, and repeating the cycle again and again? You guessed it: my family vacation. I like to refer to it as the pinnacle of my all-out tug-of-war with God over sleep. Jacob may have stayed up all night wrestling with God alone at Bethel. Not me. My all-night wrestling with God happened in an ocean-front condo in Florida, one of the most exhausting weeks of my life.

Doug and I arrived at the beach the night before Easter, tired from traveling with Nick and Anna but still anxious for some coveted rest as well as some quality time together. Anna, not yet a year old, refused to sleep in a strange crib. Nick had just turned three and wouldn't sleep alone. So we all piled into the same bed. Who said anything about rest?

By Monday morning, we were already exhausted. I had deliberately left my laptop at home, thinking I would also leave Lady Lawyer at home. No such luck. My clients started calling with more than the usual emergencies, and I had to use the outdated hotel fax machine, which made everything take twice as long. Why didn't I just bring my laptop?

I ended up working during the few hours the kids actually napped. Anna still wouldn't sleep in her crib at night. Both kids got terrible colds, I broke out in a bad case of hives after having a negative reaction to shellfish, Doug and I bickered constantly, and by the end of the week I had caught a nasty cold from the kids. So much for quality time together and rest.

The last day of vacation I wrote in my journal:

April 16

Dear Lord,
I have never been so exhausted in my life and am living on little sleep. I am sick with the kids' colds. Even though they both finally slept last night I couldn't sleep. I get to the point where I am too exhausted to sleep. I have been begging You for rest, but You have shown me that Your promise of rest comes with a condition—"Come unto Me." Show me how to focus on and obey this command. My motivation is selfish, but pure. I feel like I am too exhausted right now to be the wife and mother You have called me to be.

The next day, we barely made it to the airport on time for the flight home because—you guessed it—we had overslept. When we got home, we realized we had left our car keys at the beach. After taking a cab home, we realized we had no house key, so we had to break into our house. Doug announced that we were never traveling again with children. I was just glad to be home.

Some vacation. Back to the grind, and I needed a vacation from being on vacation. But I couldn't stop thinking about a verse I had written in my journal: "Come to me, all you who are weary and burdened, and I will give you rest. Take my yoke upon you and learn from me, for I am gentle and humble in heart, and you will find rest for your souls. For my yoke is easy and my burden is light."[1]

I was definitely weary and burdened. I didn't need sleep, I needed rest. Finding rest for my soul? A light and easy burden? It sounded too good to be true. Like the chocolate cake, God was dangling rest in front of me to no avail. What was He trying to prove anyway?

The part of the verse that kept jumping out was "Come unto me." I went back and reread my journal from the prior week.

April 12

What does it mean to come to Christ? This is the call, the first step: It starts with us. An act of our will. It is conditional upon our actions. We can't come on our own strength. We need to ask Him for the will to come. It takes discipline to come. It takes the filling of the Holy Spirit. I crave rest right now, more than anything. I am weary, burdened, and tired but I have it backwards. I won't find rest until I come to Him.

Instead of begging God for rest, I decided to just come as I was. I didn't have to clean up my act first. I didn't even have to fake it or act as if I wasn't tired. The longer I waited, the more exhausted I would become. God didn't say, "Get some sleep and call Me in the morning." He also didn't give me a formula for sleep, like getting more exercise, putting the kids on a sleep schedule, or trying to reset my body clock. He didn't even give me a pill. He just said, "Come." It's actually quite simple, but I had made it complicated.

April 21

Dear Jesus,
I'm back from vacation and can't keep up with the rat race. I was up until 2:00 a.m. last night preparing a speech. This morning I am exhausted and in need of rest but am reminded that I need to "come unto You" first. So here I am, Lord. I'm tired and stressed out, but am coming to You.

When Jesus was tired, He performed miracles. I am reminded of Christ's words to His disciples after being stalked by the crowds for several days. Everyone was exhausted, and the disciples wanted to send the crowds away, but Jesus didn't say, "I'm tired; tell them to go away until we get some rest." Instead, he said, "You give them something to eat."[2] Then He does the unthinkable. He feeds over five thousand through the lunch of a small boy. So before I decide I am too tired, done for the day, or useless in my state of exhaustion, I am reminded to check with Christ first. Tired or not, I don't want to miss out on a miracle.

TWELVE

Will I Ever Be Content?

> I know what it is to be in need, and I know what it is to have plenty. I have learned the secret of being content in any and every situation, whether well fed or hungry, whether living in plenty or in want. I can do everything through him who gives me strength.
>
> Philippians 4:12–13

We've all had one of those days. It all started in my parking garage, earlier that morning. First, you have to understand my baggage with the garage. Our building management got the bright idea that they could squeeze more money out of the parking spots if they painted the lines closer together. An average-sized vehicle can barely fit between the lines. And don't plan on being able to comfortably get out of your car without smacking the car next to you. Several times when I was pregnant, I actually had to crawl through the hatchback to get out. And I always have car filth on my suit from rubbing against the car next to me. My wagon is scratched, dented, and relatively compact. As long as I park in this garage, I have vowed that I am never getting a new car.

I drove Doug's oversized SUV to work once. I knew it was a bad idea to even attempt to drive that beast into my parking garage, especially after I had hit the side of the house, but my wagon was in the shop and I had again underestimated my limitations. I should have stuck with my instincts. You guessed it, I couldn't make the sharp turn into one of those tiny parking spots, and I ended up swiping a metal pole. Have I mentioned how much I hate driving his vehicle?

So I'm bitter about this garage to begin with. Every time I pass that metal pole on level 2, my blood starts to boil and I wonder how many other people have had their days ruined (or their spouse's day ruined) by this garage. On this particular day, there were no decent spots, so I squeezed my wagon into the best space possible. Besides, I would be leaving the garage in just a few hours for Abby's pediatrician appointment. It's not like I would have to occupy a lousy spot for the whole day.

It's always a challenge to make a 10:15 a.m. doctor appointment after spending a short morning in the office. Why had I even bothered to come to work? I would get stuck on a conference call or, worse yet, one of my senior partners would plop himself down in my office and refuse to leave. But difficult or not, I had to get a few things off my desk that morning and I managed to make a clean exit, putting me back in the garage just before 10:00 a.m. I immediately noticed a note on my windshield. *How unusual,* I thought. *It's not even Christmas, and my secret Santa is already leaving me letters.* Or maybe it was one of my friends pretending to be the Easter Bunny—Easter was just around the corner, and I was sure it would be some kind of encouraging note.

I reached on my windshield to find anything but a word of encouragement. It read, "Park in the lines, you idiot!" I laughed out loud. I have never been proud of my driving, but no one can take away my sense of humor. I had more important things to do with my day than get upset about a nasty note.

I quickly forgot about the note and raced to pick up Abby for her appointment, where her pediatrician would undoubtedly diagnose another ear infection. On the way to the doctor's office, I was sitting at an intersection and minding my own business when another driver laid on her horn. Unbeknownst to me, I was blocking the entrance to the bank, and she was trying to make a turn. No, I wasn't talking on my cell phone or daydreaming, and I wasn't even multitasking. Rather than waiting for the light to turn green or giving me a friendly toot, she laid on her horn and gave me an obscene gesture.

I really had no incentive to reciprocate the gesture, but at this point in the day I started to wonder why people are so rude. Even more perplexing is fathoming who has time to be rude. Someone in my parking garage had to pull out a blank sheet of paper and handwrite me a note and place it on my windshield just to tell me I'm an idiot. Did he or she really think that note was going to make me a better driver? I don't have time to write notes to people I don't know about problems I can't solve in a parking garage I didn't design. Don't people have better things to do with their time?

After the pediatrician, Abby and I were waiting in line at the pharmacy for her antibiotic when a woman swooped in front of me and announced, "There's a line, you know." I bit my tongue and smiled politely. The woman looked about my age. There wasn't even a line formed, yet she expected me to have mental telepathy and know otherwise. Who wants to hover around the pharmacy desk in a crammed line while the pharmacist explains the unpleasant side effects of someone else's medicine? Not me. The pharmacy desk has a big sign that says, "Please, for privacy concerns, only one person approach the pharmacy at a time." Of course, this stops people from making a line. I was just trying to follow the rules.

I realize this woman wasn't trying to ruin my day, but I had already been called an idiot, honked and sworn at, and I had a sick baby with an ear infection and a conference call that I had to get on in about fifteen minutes. Poor Abby was probably going to have to wait for her first dose of medicine until after my conference call. And then I was going to have to try to work from home the rest of the day, which meant I would get absolutely nothing done.

So, by Anna's bedtime, I was putting her to bed when she asked, "Why are you mad at me?" At first, I didn't know what she was talking about.

"What do you mean, honey?" I hadn't yelled at her. I hadn't put her in time-out. And we had just finished reading one of her favorite stories.

She went on, "Why do you have your mean face on tonight?"

Unfortunately, she was right. I hadn't cracked a smile since I had gotten home. I had let the day get the best of me, and now I was taking it out on my children. It was only Tuesday, and I was more than ready for the weekend.

The Weekend … Finally

By the time the weekend rolled around, Abby was finally feeling better, and I decided to take the girls to Barnes & Noble for a special Saturday morning outing to buy a couple of books for Easter. Anna and Abby wanted a cookie and hot chocolate, and I got my usual double-tall, nonfat latte and found a magazine, and we planted ourselves at a comfortable spot at the café. The girls were better-behaved than usual—no fighting, screaming, or whining—and they were even taking turns talking. Anna kept asking if tomorrow was Easter, and Abby kept repeating everything Anna said, a little louder and with just the right amount of inflection. I reminded them that the hot chocolate was really hot, and to hold it with two hands. Anna proclaimed that it was the best hot chocolate she had ever had in her life and I thought to myself, life just doesn't get much better than this. Here I am, hanging out in a coffee shop with my two beautiful girls. The thought of it warmed my heart as I sipped my latte. It hadn't been such a bad week after all. Thank God for the weekend.

Then I heard a man yelling at someone behind me. I couldn't completely understand him, but he was swearing, and obviously upset. So I turned around. He was packing up his things on the table behind me, but there was no one around him. Then it occurred to me. He was yelling at *me.* I looked right at him, but he wouldn't even look back. Instead, he stomped across the café and found an empty table on the other side. But what had I done to him? Why was this middle-aged, bearded man full of such anger and rage?

Then it occurred to me. He was a MECH. Otherwise known as a Middle-Aged Elitist Child Hater. All of a sudden, I wanted to put on my lawyer cape and squash him like a bug. Not only was he a MECH, he was a leech! He was reading some technical manual that he definitely wasn't going to purchase, and he wasn't even buying a refill for his coffee. As a paying customer, I had every right to be in that café with my children. We had already bought two books, a cookie, two hot chocolates, plus my latte. He's too cheap to even buy the book he was reading, yet he wants me to move so that he can have some space! Obviously, he was jealous of me and my beautiful children, and he probably knows deep down that he will never have children of his own because no one wants to marry him. Or worse yet, he's probably going through a midlife crisis, left his wife and children, and drives a red, two-seater sports car with no room for car seats. I wanted to give him a piece of my mind, but Devoted Mommy gained control, we quietly finished the cookie and hot chocolate, and we left the café without encounter. After all, I wasn't going to let a MECH ruin a perfect Saturday with my girls. Or was I?

I was still mad when I got home. The nerve of him! I should head back to the store and show him what a real tantrum looks like. He thought the girls were loud—wait until he sees them in full-blown meltdown mode. I could arrange an encounter he would never forget!

Then I remembered what life was like before I had children. I used to look at those mothers with strollers who blocked the aisles in stores and think, "Don't you think about anyone else in the world but yourself? Other people are trying to shop here!" And I used to go to the bookstore to find a quiet spot just to study, and I even got annoyed a few times when mothers brought in their loud obnoxious children.

Of course my girls hadn't been the slightest bit obnoxious, but maybe I had the MECH all wrong. Maybe he has a house full of kids at home and was just trying to get out for a morning. Okay, probably not. But maybe, like me, he had had a lousy week and he just needed some peace and quiet. Had I become one of those self-absorbed mothers who thinks the world revolves around her children?

So after I got home and cooled off, I decided to pray for the MECH. I prayed that he would deal with his issues, whatever they may be, and that his anger would bring him closer to God. And I thanked God for showing me that sometimes I get a little too self-righteous and I need to take a good look in the mirror.

Spoiled Rotten

If I'm really honest, I have to admit that most days I fit right in with the MECH and the other rude folks who leave notes on my car and honk at the light. Maybe I don't write anonymous notes, give obscene gestures, or thrown tantrums in coffee shops, but I'm always mad at someone. Starting with the office. I complain when I'm busy at work—but not nearly as much as I complain when I'm slow. The associate on the project didn't find the right research. The filing was late. Someone forgot to tell me about a meeting. I'm late for an interview. My realization rate is too low. My billing rate is too high. My email is down again. I keep getting put on hold when I call the help desk. We don't have enough staffing to meet the deadline. And most clients wanted an answer yesterday. Good is never good enough.

It's not like things are any better at home. I'm mad at Doug for not helping me put the kids to bed. "Do I have to do everything myself around here?" I say it under my breath, but just loud enough for him to hear. And he forgot to call about Nick's hockey registration again even though I reminded him ten times. I'm mad at the kids because they won't listen to me. Nick and Anna keep teasing Abby about her big-girl underwear, and Abby keeps saying the word *poop,* which makes Nick and Anna howl with laughter, and no one is going to get settled down before bed and I'm going to be up half the night again trying to get everything done.

Then I start into my personal pity party. *You haven't held my job, been married to my husband, raised my kids, or paid my mortgage. No one understands, and I'm getting pretty tired of holding it all together myself.*

Not to mention I'm getting more high maintenance by the day. I expect the finest food, the best accommodations, and the best price. Haven't you ever heard of customer service? And the smallest things set me off these days—a low tank of gas, a line at the grocery store, Abby's tantrums, the neighbor kids parked in front of my house, and, yes, even spilled milk.

Doug joins me and complains, "I can't wait until she's out of diapers" and "If we could only skip the terrible twos." This makes me even more upset, and I yell at him for trying to rush my last baby. But then I catch myself doing the same thing.

"A year from now, we'll have cut our day-care costs in half," or, "In five years at least we'll have some money saved for college."

Bills. Child care. Kids' activities. Dinners out. More bills. Gifts. Travel. Remodeling. Then we start freaking out about saving for retirement. Will we have enough? It's completely irrational. We're going to work harder and longer so that when we're too old or sick to really enjoy ourselves we don't have to worry about money. Don't get me wrong—I'm all for delayed gratification, but whatever happened to daily bread?

Our church regularly says the Lord's Prayer in worship. I keep getting stuck on daily bread.

"Give us this day our daily bread."

It doesn't say give us bread for next year or even next week. And we're supposed to request bread on this day—apparently the same day we eat it. God knew what He was doing when He told the Israelites to take just enough manna for one day at a time. If I were an Israelite in the wilderness, I would probably try to store too much manna, and it would get worms. Sometimes I wonder, *Why is it so hard for me to be content with what I have?*

I know that God is speaking to me in the midst of my pity party. "You're spoiled rotten, Susan. Get over yourself, okay?" He says it a little nicer than that, but I get the point.

Then, when I pretend like I don't hear Him, He shows me other people in my life who are hurting. Often they are mothers, and when I look at their journeys it reminds me to "be content with what you have."[1] I don't know why I can't see this myself—why I can't be not only content but completely thankful for everyone and everything in my life—but sometimes it helps to put myself in someone else's shoes.

A Matter of Perspective

God uses Big-Hearted Betty, the first woman who ever watched my children, on a regular basis to show me just how much I have to be thankful for. She always tells me to enjoy these times and appreciate life while my kids are young. She should know. Her world as a single mother changed when her middle son, Mike, was seventeen. She blames herself for letting him go out one night with a group of friends and always says, "If only I would have stopped him." Mike never reached his eighteenth birthday because of a fatal car accident, and Betty has never gotten over the heartache. As any mother would, she always asks God why He let this happen. She was even at a prayer meeting the night before his death. Yet she doesn't blame God; she still blames herself.

Shortly after Betty's oldest boy, Terry, turned forty, his cancer set in. Terry died shortly after his forty-first birthday, and since his death Betty's ache is too deep to even talk about. How many mothers have lost two of their three sons to untimely deaths? The stress has nearly killed her, and had she not fought so hard to live she would have died of a broken heart. It's really too much heartache for one woman to bear. But Betty still continues to fight, and she loves little children more than anything because they remind her of better days.

So when Big-Hearted Betty gives me advice, I try to listen. She always says to me, "Susan, these are the best years of your life. I'd do anything to have my kids back again."

When I look at my kids, I'm just thankful to have them and hold them. I forget about my parking garage, rude drivers, and the MECH. I even forget about how much I have to do at work, or my need to save more for retirement. And when I start to have a pity party, I'm reminded of Big-Hearted Betty.

On Mother's Day, the kids woke me up and gave me cards and homemade presents in bed. It was better than Christmas morning. Nick and Anna had made me a scrapbook of baby pictures and family photos, which Nick had titled *The Book of Memories.* I barely noticed that the glue was so thick that the pictures were lumpy and wet. And I didn't care that they had used all the rejects that didn't make it into the family album. It was the nicest gift I had ever received.

Then I thought about Big-Hearted Betty. Would anyone take the time to make her feel special on Mother's Day? Her sons would be looking down from heaven and smiling, but I still had to call her. But when? After presents and breakfast we were off to church. Then lunch. Five loads of laundry. Housecleaning for guests. I started to get emails from work around midday. (Who in her right mind works on Mother's Day?) I ignored the emails through dinner but then returned a few messages. More cleanup and playtime. I had to get the kids in bed early for school. Baths. Stories. Prayers. I looked at my watch. I had forgotten to call Big-Hearted Betty. Better late than never, I gave her a call after the kids went to bed. She picked up the phone and started to cry. She had spent the day alone. No phone calls. No cards. No scrapbooks.

After I hung up the phone, I shed a few tears and thanked God again for using Big-Hearted Betty to show me how much I really have. Like the apostle Paul, Big-Hearted Betty knows what it's like to live in plenty and to have need.

My children also help me put things in perspective on a regular basis. Like Anna. Anna is the most content child I know. It doesn't take much to make her happy. A blank sheet of paper and markers. Time alone in her room. Listening to music. Going to the park. Mommy picking her up from school. Playing beauty shop, and doing Mom's hair. She rarely asks for more, and she'd rather spend time than money. Last year at Disney World, I took her to all the shows and paid to have her dressed up like a princess. By the second day, she was tired and ready to go back to the hotel. So instead of dragging her to more shows, rides, and long lines, we went back to the hotel and lay down. She turned all the lights off, put on her own show with flashlights, and then we went swimming. It was one of the best days we had together in a long time.

When we got home, everyone asked her about Disney. *What was your favorite part? Did you get to see all the princesses?* Anna announced to everyone that her favorite part of the trip was—you guessed it—"swimming at the hotel with Mom." In other words, we could have rented a hotel down the street with a swimming pool and spent the day together. Some lessons come with a heavy price tag.

I'm sure when Anna is sixteen, she's going to have a list of demands and I'm going to look back and remember the trip to Disney. When she says, "Mom, I really want my own car," I'm going to respond, "Anna, I can remember the days when you were happy just staying home and playing beauty shop." Then I'm going to remind her about the trip to Disney, and how she was more content spending time than money.

I'm sure her life won't always be this simple, but I pray that she would always have her spirit of contentment. Just watching her reminds me how far I have to go.

Maybe you have a child in your life like Anna, who reminds you to be thankful for the little things, like spending time together. Or maybe you have a friend like Big-Hearted Betty, a friend who has had a journey much harder than yours who helps put your own life in perspective. For whatever reason, many of us working mothers think that nobody has it quite as hard as we do and sometimes we forget to be content, no matter the circumstances.

THIRTEEN

Who Has Time to Be Superwoman?

> But do not forget one thing, dear friends: With the Lord a day is like a thousand years, and a thousand years are like a day.
>
> 2 Peter 3:8

What would I do if I had an entire day off? I mean totally off: no work, no activities, no cooking, no laundry, no carpool, no shopping, no gatherings, no errands. What would it really be like to have nothing, absolutely nothing, to do? I can't even let myself go there.

For now, my days "off" are reserved for my family. Have I mentioned that I have no social life? I used to make plans on nights and weekends and stay out late. I would write letters to old friends, make new friends, and organize gatherings with zeal. I was raised with a clan of sisters, after all. The more the merrier.

So why have I become antisocial? I'm incredibly stingy with my time. These days, I'm grumpy if my nights and weekends are packed with too much to do. My ideal weekend? Stay at home and do nothing.

The reason? I've simply run out of time.

Everything is a cost-benefit analysis. If I exercise, I can't eat lunch. If I eat lunch, I have to work late. If I write, I give up sleep. If I take Abby to her doctor's appointment, I have to work late tomorrow. If I go to Bible study, I give up time with Doug at night. If I take a day off work, I always have to make up billable hours.

Everyone seems to want my time, including me.

Me and My Laptop

I really want a pedicure. And I never have time to get my hair colored. By the time I drive to the salon, wait in line, get my hair cut and colored, and drive home, it's a minimum investment of three hours. Who has three hours to spare? Not me. Which is why I wait until the last possible moment to get color. My roots are completely gray (not entirely a bad thing when you're a trial lawyer). But sooner or later, I have to break down. I'm too vain. One of the great things about being the youngest sister is that everyone gets old before me. When I was little, I always wanted to be the oldest. But now that I'm older, I realize there are certain advantages to being younger. Like being the last one to get wrinkles. And, no, I'm not planning to show my gray any time soon.

So I squeeze a few hours out of my workday for the salon and put a meeting on my calendar that says, "Meeting at HS re: H&B." It sounds important. Translation? "Meeting at Hair Salon regarding Hair and Brows." I'm not about to tell my clients I can't make a meeting because I have to get my brows waxed.

Without exception, I'm the only person who brings a laptop into the salon. Most of the other women are reading *Cosmo* or a trashy novel. I get a few stares and I wonder, am I the only one here who is pressed for time? Apparently so. I try to plan it so that my conference calls fall during the forty-five-minute break where my color soaks in, otherwise the stylist is beyond annoyed when I'm on the phone while she's trying to color my hair. The other problem is that the goopy chemical solution always cakes around my ears and leaves a stain on my phone. Otherwise, the salon is a perfect place for a conference call. It's relatively quiet, no one bothers me, and it relieves my anxiety to know that I am not wasting time after all. At least I can bill for it.

If I'm running ahead of schedule, I'll take the time and get my brows waxed. After all, I'm already there and I can kill two birds with one stone. I absolutely hate tweezing my eyebrows. It's right behind ironing and washing windows. But I figured out that it's not really worth my time to go to the salon just for my brows when they will just grow back in a few weeks. Every time I get them waxed, I get the same guilt trip: "You really should come in every three weeks, especially with your Mediterranean condition." Instead, I'm patiently waiting for the unibrow to become high fashion. But I can spare the extra fifteen minutes when I'm already at the salon, and it's really nice when my brows aren't connected—at least for a few weeks.

One of my friends has the same problem with her brows. Her secret? She tweezes them in the car and claims she'll never go back. Not only does it save her time, but her brows look better because the outdoor lighting is far superior. So I put my tweezers in my purse and thought about giving it a try. The only problem? I'm already too busy in the car.

Another thing I don't have time for? Talking on the phone. I used to think Doug was rude because he never answers our home phone. These days, I have to agree. Lady Lawyer is already strapped to her phone all day. Who has time for personal calls? Email may be impersonal, but it is easier, faster, and—most importantly—done according to *my* schedule. This is one of the reasons I'm addicted to Facebook. It actually saves me time. In a matter of thirty seconds, my news feed tells me who's had a bad day, who's changing jobs, and who's coming into town this weekend. I don't have to talk to anyone, and I don't have to answer messages unless I want to. And no one thinks I'm ignoring them, because I can post about how busy I am with the kids or what I'm doing at work, and I'm actually saving my friends time because they don't have to call me either to know the intimate details of my life. They can just read about it like everyone else.

Okay, Facebook may be a little impersonal, and I know you can't have real relationships solely over the Internet. But there's something to say for the convenience and efficiency of mass communication, especially for a working mother. And while I know I probably waste time on Facebook, being able to respond to messages or read updates when it's convenient for me—like when everyone else is sleeping—makes me feel like I have greater control over my time, even though I probably don't. Unfortunately, some of my friends will never join Facebook, and they always call at the worst time.

As much as I love Big-Hearted Betty, she always calls in the evenings when I'm trying to put the kids to bed or on Saturday mornings when the family has already been apart all week and we just need some down time together. I can't hang up on her—we're the closest thing to family she has. She's lonely, and she just wants to talk. She can carry a conversation by herself—it's not like it takes much effort on my part—I just have to listen. But even listening takes time, so after I listen to her for a few minutes I usually interrupt her in midsentence and find my exit.

After I get off the phone with Big-Hearted Betty, Encouraging Amy calls. I don't answer. No, I haven't yet been able to convince her (or any of my sisters) to join Facebook. We can't have a superficial conversation, so it's a minimum of twenty minutes every time we talk. And I don't have twenty minutes. I really want to talk to her too. I need to hear her encouraging voice, and I want to hear about her kindergarten class, Kaitlyn's cheerleading camp, and the struggles and excitement of starting to plan for her first child to enter college. Instead, I ignore the call. I can email her later.

I don't even have time to call my own mother on a Saturday morning. Last year, I sent her birthday card a week late. I still feel terrible about it. I had every intention of getting it in the mail sooner, but I was traveling the week before, and when the weekend rolled around I completely lost track of time. I would send her one of those automatic email cards, but she's not even on the Internet, let alone Facebook.

Who has time to keep up with all the birthday cards anyway? I keep up as best I can. Kids come first, followed by parents and sisters. Forget friends and acquaintances. Brothers-in-law fell off the list about ten years ago. Doug doesn't really care about birthday cards, but the kids and I still try to remember to do something special every time his birthday rolls around.

Being a Multitaskaholic

When Doug turned forty, I knew I couldn't wait until the last minute to pull his gift together, and I wanted him to be surprised. I thought long and hard about what I could give him. The only thing he really wanted was a flat-screen TV for our bedroom. The thought of it made me shudder. I just couldn't bring myself to do it. I had to come up with something that wouldn't keep me up at night or drive me absolutely crazy. So I came up with the best gift I could think of. Time. Doug loves nothing more than my time. I planned an elaborate trip that would be a complete surprise.

The plan? His mother and sister would arrive after dinner on Thursday evening for cake and ice cream. I'd invite a few of his friends to stop by, then I would spring on him that we were leaving in the morning for a three-day trip to an oceanfront resort. He hates surprises. But this was different. What could go wrong?

Lady Lawyer planned the trip from my office. My first mistake. Come to think of it, I think I planned the trip while I was on a conference call. Second mistake. I'm what they call a multitaskaholic.

Doug opened all of his gifts, and my gift was last. When he opened our plane tickets, he looked at the date and time. You guessed it, I had booked the wrong flights. Nonrefundable and nontransferable tickets. He really wasn't very excited once we figured out the fee to rebook the flights would be more than the cost of the entire trip.

So we cancelled the trip and stayed home. The next day, my in-laws went home early, I took the day off work, and we took the kids to a pumpkin festival. I got sick on the Ferris wheel and vowed never to surprise Doug again. In a moment of weakness, I told him to just go and buy that flat-screen TV he really wanted for our bedroom. So Doug got his TV, and I got sick on the Ferris wheel. Multitasking has its limits. So much for the gift of time.

I've thought about starting my own chapter of Multitaskaholics Anonymous. "Sorry kids, I can't be home for dinner tonight, I'm on my way to my MA meeting." But the last thing I need is more time away from the kids, so I'll have to cope for now.

At the office I know people are talking about my addiction behind my back. "You know, one of these days she's going to push the limit too far. Have you seen her emails while she's on conference calls? You can always tell when she's multitasking because she just agrees with everything you say, which *never* happens when she's paying attention."

They certainly have a point. At least my law partner, Harvard Bill, had the guts to attempt an intervention. He tried to persuade me that there's no such thing as multitasking—"Your brain just switches gears and can focus on only one thing at a time." He sounded convincing, and he twisted my arm to seek professional help. Some college professor had studied the impacts of multitasking in the workplace, and he was speaking to a group of attorneys about the ethical implications of multitasking. I agreed I needed the help, so I signed up for the seminar and had every intention of attending.

The only problem? Something came up at the last minute, I was in the middle of multitasking, and I missed it.

Slowing Down

Another indicator of my constant hurry? Speeding tickets. Unfortunately, I've learned the hard way that even Superwoman can't fly, and I have my share of citations to prove it. Most of my speeding tickets are from the morning, when I'm on my way to work, taking the kids to school. I'm always late, and I'm always in a hurry. Come to think of it, I never got speeding tickets until after I became a working mother. Every time I get behind the wheel, Lady Lead Foot just takes over. For this reason alone, I will never have a bumper sticker on my car that has anything to do with my faith. Jesus already has a bad name in enough circles. He doesn't need my help.

It was one thing when I got a ticket for going forty miles per hour in a twenty-five-miles-per-hour zone. I didn't even see the sign. It's a completely commercial district, and no one would know the speed limit was only twenty-five miles per hour unless, like me, you get caught. The police officer also zapped me for not having a front license plate. How was I supposed to know it was a legal requirement? What does he think I am, a lawyer or something?

Then there were the highway tickets—going a "little" over the speed limit when I thought I was just keeping up with traffic.

Sometimes Lady Lead Foot just takes control, and before I know it the red lights are flashing. I really didn't think I had a problem until the school bus incident. It's one thing to get a speeding ticket, but a five-hundred-dollar fine, a potential license suspension, and up to sixty days in jail? What was I thinking? Sometimes, when the gentle whisper doesn't work, God just has to smack me over the head to get my attention.

It all happened on a Thursday morning around 8:00 a.m. I was taking Abby to preschool and, you guessed it, I was running late. I came to a long line of cars just sitting in front of me. What could be the hold up? I decided to just pass them.

When I came to the front of the line I saw a school bus. I panicked, put my head down, and put the pedal to the metal. At that point, what were my choices anyway? I couldn't exactly stop in the middle of the passing lane. Besides, there were no children around. One of the cars gave me a loud honk (I would later learn this was my neighbor) and Lady Lead Foot took over. This was a lot worse than a speeding ticket. I was completely ashamed. At least Abby wasn't old enough to understand, and no harm was done. Or so I thought.

The next morning at seven-thirty, someone was knocking at our front door. I looked outside and saw a police car. My heart sank. They were coming for me. It served me right. I should have learned my lesson with the speeding tickets. But no, I always have to push the envelope. This time, I had really done it. I'd made a lot of mistakes over the years, but I never thought I'd spend time in prison. Incarcerated Mommy was not going to be able to take very good care of the children. At least Lady Lawyer gets to come home at night. I couldn't bear the thought of my children seeing me in prison. And what would I say to my Sunday school students? I thought I could never get fired from teaching Sunday school, but acts of moral turpitude are an automatic disqualifier. At least some time in prison would give me time to finish the book. I guess it could be worse.

Doug invited the police officer inside. First mistake. Every lawyer knows that you never talk to the police, but Doug apparently wasn't listening to me when I gave him the crash course in criminal law. The police were in our living room.

"Suz, get down here!" Doug yelled. I was hiding upstairs.

"Honey, I'm not dressed, and I just got out of the shower. Tell the officer good-bye and we need to get the kids to school." Doug still wouldn't listen. He started to argue with the police officer, and I knew there must be trouble.

Then I heard the officer say, "I have an affidavit from the bus driver, and she spotted a forty-year-old white male, driving a silver wagon that matches your license plate, passing her vehicle while the lights were flashing."

Doug responded, "That's impossible. I never even drive that car. Suz, get down here!"

I was not about to go downstairs. The officer left, and I didn't know whether to laugh or cry. *Doug* had gotten cited.

So I did what most responsible citizens would do. I hired an attorney. In the end, I took a plea and even put the citation in my name. After all, my insurance rates are already shot.

Looking back, I guess I'm thankful that I got caught. I'm thankful that no children were crossing. I'm thankful that the driver called me in, and my neighbor had the guts to honk. I'm thankful that God reached down to me. Sometimes subtle just doesn't work. I'm happily driving the speed limit now, especially in school zones. Cars still honk at me, but usually it's because I'm going too slow. I'm tempted to roll down my window and say, "Hey, stop honking at me. You'd go slowly too if you had my driving record." But instead I just smile and let them pass me. Some people just have to learn the hard way. And I'm really thankful I didn't have to spend any time in jail. I hear the food is awful.

I really believe that God used the school bus incident to slow me down that day. Not only did I need to slow down in the car, I needed to take a deep breath and stop rushing around in just about every area of my life. Besides, I'm really enjoying the extra time in the car to pray. Who am I chasing anyway?

Okay, God, I've really screwed up this time. I'm so sorry for being in a hurry and putting other people—especially children—in danger. Thanks that I didn't have to go to jail, and forgive me for having to learn lessons the hard way. Thanks for making me slow down.

Eternity

We all have time for the things that are important. The truth is, I have lots of time. God knew what He was doing when He put twenty-four hours in a day, seven days in a week, and 365 days in a year. In fact, according to some studies, my generation has more disposable time than any generation in history. We may choose to book our schedules with more stuff than our parents ever dreamed of—like long days at the office, kids' activities every night of the week, and social calendars that give us new photos to post on Facebook—but at the end of the day it doesn't mean we have less time.

I once heard a pastor say that Christians have the one thing that everyone in the world is longing for. Time. We have the gift of eternal life. I had never thought of it in these terms. In other words, our time will never run out. It seems too good to be true, but then I look at Jesus. Jesus doesn't appear to multitask. He does one thing at a time, and He does it right. Somehow He's able to give me His undivided attention all the time. It's completely divine.

I can't tell you the last time I gave anyone my undivided attention.

Eternity will be different. I can sit and talk with Big-Hearted Betty for hours. Anna and I can have a tea party for a hundred years, and I'll never tell Nick to hurry up and finish putting his shoes on so we can get to school on time, because we'll never be late. There won't be any billable hours in heaven. Doug and I can finally celebrate his fortieth birthday without the flat-screen TV, and I'll get a pedicure every weekend. I won't get any more speeding tickets, because I'll never be in a hurry. And my eyebrows will never grow together, unless of course it's high fashion. Just thinking about eternity helps me slow down.

FOURTEEN

Devoted Mommy

> Her children arise and call her blessed; her husband also, and he praises her: "Many women do noble things, but you surpass them all."
>
> Proverbs 31:28–29

What does it mean to be Devoted Mommy? I use this term loosely, but deep down it's really what I want to be known for most.

When I think about the high calling of raising children I get completely overwhelmed. One thing's for sure, I need lots of help—which is why I constantly read books on parenting. I'm not sure I've learned anything, other than no one has really figured it out. Typically, I buy a new book and read the first few chapters with zeal. Then a range of doubts and discouragement overcome me. *I've tried this before and it doesn't work.* Or worse, *Maybe this would have worked at the time, but I've already blown it.*

Then the guilt starts in. As my kids get older, I'm losing more and more control. According to the experts, the kids watch too much TV, eat too much junk, and make too many choices. Anna shouldn't be allowed to wear Hannah Montana T-shirts; Nick should be limited to twenty minutes a day of video games; and the entire household should not revolve around Abby's latest tantrum. Maybe I should have had them all on that rigid feeding schedule at birth after all.

Lessons from My Mother

I don't think my mother put me on a rigid feeding schedule, so maybe there's still hope. She read Bible stories to me every night and taught me to read from the King James Version. My second grade teacher wondered why I was always using words like *thou* and *thee* and quoting from the Twenty-third Psalm. We were in church on Sunday morning, Sunday evening, and Wednesday evening, and I wasn't allowed to miss Sunday school unless I was deathly ill. But she never tried to control my interests or my friends, and she never got rigid about theology. Instead, she modeled an authentic faith and would get tears in her eyes every time she talked about how much she loved Jesus. Bedtime prayers could last up to twenty minutes. In addition to praying for family and friends, she always prayed for people she didn't even know, souls yet to be saved, and last but not least, the peace of Jerusalem. I remember thinking to myself some evenings, *Where does she come up with all this stuff? Doesn't she just want to go to sleep?* One time I even asked her, "Mom, why do you always pray for the peace of Jerusalem?" After all, hasn't there always been fighting in the Mideast? Doe she really think her prayers are going to change thousands of years of turmoil?

Her answer? Psalm 122:6: "Pray for the peace of Jerusalem." She's more concerned about doing the right thing and leaves the outcome to God.

Unlike my mother, I don't have my kids in church three times a week. We're lucky to make it to Sunday school on time, and we can just forget about perfect attendance. But I still try to keep a ritual of bedtime stories and prayers. Unfortunately my prayers often last about twenty seconds, and lots of times we don't get beyond our own family, let alone people we don't know or distant lands. I usually forget to pray for the peace of Jerusalem.

Now that I have children of my own, you'd think my mother would give me a bunch of unsolicited advice. But she doesn't. That's what older sisters are for. So I watch her, very closely, and Devoted Mommy tries to model her the best I can.

Sometimes I ask her, "How did you do it, Mom?"

She gives me the same answer every time, in the King James Version, of course: "Train up a child in the way he should go: and when he is old, he will not depart from it."[1]

I listen for a couple of reasons. First, she's my mother. Second, her advice is so much simpler than all those parenting books. Simple is good right now.

I've watched her for years. Rising early in the morning to have time alone with God. Raising five daughters. Managing a household. Being patient with my father on his own faith journey. Battling illness and depression. Overcoming cancer. Running circles around her grandchildren. I wish she had a formula I could package, and I always tell her, "Mom, if I can be half the mother you've been, I'll be satisfied."

She also taught me that the most powerful tool of a parent is unconditional love. When I was fourteen, I got busted skinny-dipping at church camp in the middle of the night under questionable circumstances. Unfortunately, my youth pastor called my mother the next morning to give a full report of my indiscretions. I apologized through my tears and begged her not to tell my father. She never breathed a word. No questions. Just complete and total forgiveness. I'm sure she got on her knees and even shed a few tears in the process, but she never let me see her flinch.

Lessons from Trusting Tracy

Some women are born to be mothers. Other women, like me, didn't have any maternal instincts until after we had children. Jock Jill used to say that she had the maternal instincts of a rattlesnake, but nature quickly took over after she had her daughter and now she wonders what life was like before she was a mother. Sassy Shelly wasn't even planning to have Sam, but he changed her life forever. Soon after his birth she was determined to beat her biological clock and quickly birthed three more children.

Some women want to be mothers more than anything in the world, including some of my friends who don't have children of their own. Trusting Tracy is one of those women. Not only does she want to be a mother, she was made to be a mother. She's had a successful career and at one point she even had a family of her own. A family that was taken away after a difficult divorce and a stepdaughter who will no longer call her mama. My heart breaks sometimes when I watch her with my own children. She is patient, loving, creative, and even crafty. She turns old newspapers into art projects and even showed Anna how to make a homemade dictionary with letters and pictures. She's so much more natural at motherhood than just about anyone I know. Which is why I really can't understand why God hasn't given her the one thing in life she really wants.

We all know someone who wants children so badly that it hurts so much to even imagine what she must be thinking and feeling. Some of our sisters and friends are going through tedious and expensive fertility treatments, and others are waiting for years and saving money for adoptions. Before I was a mother, I used to think women obsessed with procreating just needed to move on. Now I understand why they don't give up. And I know from talking to these friends that the last thing they want is for people like me to feel sorry for them. The wait is bad enough. The last thing you need is some fertile woman like me patronizing you or telling you she knows how bad you really have it. No, I really don't understand and I probably never will. So instead we listen and support our friends and pray that we will all become stronger women together.

So we pray for Trusting Tracy as we anxiously await the adoption of her daughter, Jaina. We don't know who Jaina is yet, and we may not meet her for a few years. But we know that she and Anna and Abby will be great friends. Tracy will take them to the park together while I am stuck on conference calls, and they will make lots of doll clothes together and dress up like princesses and make homemade dictionaries.

I recently asked Tracy how she waits patiently for Jaina. How do you keep your sanity when you know your daughter is out there, also waiting for you, but you can't yet go to her? This leads to a long, philosophical discussion of what it means to trust God, and Trusting Tracy explains that she finally let go when she realized the Christian life is most like a river. Instead of trying to swim upstream, you go with the current and let go. Trusting Tracy is going to make a great mommy, and I'm thankful that I get to stand by her as she waits for her daughter.

Bedtime Stories

Given that I'm gone most days, Devoted Mommy reserves nighttime for prayers and Bible stories with the kids. Bedtime is sacred and some days our only time alone. The only other place we're alone on a regular basis is the car, one of the only other spots I have a captive audience. So we talk about what we're learning in Sunday school, sing spiritual songs, and we pray when the traffic gets too heavy or the other cars honk at us. At least at bedtime it's relatively quiet, and there are no honking cars.

One night at the beginning of first grade, Nick and I were in his room getting ready to say prayers. He told me he didn't want to pray. When I asked him why, he said he was afraid his friends would hear him. I smiled gently, kissed him on the forehead, and explained to him that he doesn't have to be ashamed when he prays, but it's okay if he doesn't want to pray out loud. God can even hear our thoughts.

Nick has lots of good questions and has decided that he wants to be a scientist. In the back of my mind, I worry about how he will grapple with science and faith, but I encourage him to pursue science and even signed him up for "Mad Science" classes after school.

Nick asks me questions like, *How do we get to heaven?* I give him a long explanation by explaining Christ's death on the cross, the propitiation of sin, and the acceptance of forgiveness. He listens intently but then asks again. He is literally asking a different question: *How* do we get to heaven—by bus, by plane, by magic carpet, by time travel, or by space shuttle? I don't have these answers. I simply tell him that God takes us, but I can tell that my answers don't always satisfy him.

Another favorite question of Nick's is, *How old is Jesus?* My response is that He's always been with God the Father. Nick replies, "How did He become a baby?" This conversation goes on for some time, and I try to explain to Nick that even though Jesus was born in Bethlehem, He existed prior to being born in human form. These are complicated concepts that even I don't understand. For this reason, I always put Nick to bed last. That gives us plenty of time to sort through these issues without interruption from his younger sisters.

Anna doesn't ask as many questions. She's much more practical about her faith and is more interested in the here and now. She asks things like, *Why did God make mosquitoes?* I want to explain to her that the world is not the way God originally intended and that things will be perfect in heaven. But I never seem to have the right words, she gets more confused, and we decide we'll just ask God when we get to heaven. She likes that answer better.

Abby insists on praying out loud rather dramatically. She seems to pray more than anyone else in the family, but I fear that it's because she simply likes to hear herself talk. She prays for everyone in our extended family by name, thanks God for the sun, moon, and stars, and then tells Him about her day and her view of the world, and then she proceeds to thank Him again for the same things, in case He didn't hear her the first time. Usually one of us has to cut her off at the dinner table before our food gets cold.

Nick is always worried about his younger sisters' moral and spiritual development. I constantly have to remind him that God put his parents in charge of his sisters, not him, but he still tries to tell me how to discipline Anna or when to put Abby in time-out. When Nick was four, he came to me and told me that Anna had a lot of sin in her heart. I tried not to laugh, and I explained to him that Anna is younger than he, and God is patient with all of us despite our mistakes.

Sometimes, God speaks to my children in the most unexpected places. Like Target. Nick and Anna were bickering while I was shopping—nothing more than the usual sibling rivalry, but this time Nick gave me a look of terror. Something was really bothering him. "What is it, Nick?" I asked him.

"I can't tell you here, not in front of Anna," he replied. I immediately assumed the worst. Anna had done something terribly wrong, right under my nose, and I had missed it. She's always pushing Nick's buttons, and this time she must have pushed him over the edge. I asked him a second time what had happened, but he still wanted to wait until we got home.

I could only imagine the level of moral turpitude, but was at least glad he didn't want to embarrass Anna, nor cause more drama in the middle of Target. On the way home, he couldn't hold it in any longer. He starting crying and spilled his guts in the car. "Sometimes the Devil tries to make me punch Anna." Then he looked at me and said, "Are you going to kick me out of the house?"

I didn't know whether to laugh or cry. What kind of mother did he think I was anyway? So I explained to him that he wouldn't get kicked out of the house and that even Jesus was tempted. The important thing is not giving in. And even when we screw up, God still forgives us.

Cool Mom Is a Hot Mom

Even though I want to teach my kids about God and have lots of spiritual conversations, I really want them to think I'm cool. In fact, if they don't think I'm cool, they're going to tune me out completely by the fifth grade, or even sooner. So while bedtime is reserved for prayers and stories, I try to squeeze in fun whenever we can. Anna and I love to go in her room, shut the door, and blast Hannah Montana as loud as we can while Anna and Abby put on a show. We put on blonde wigs, wear heavy makeup, and use a karaoke player with microphones. Abby knows all the words to "Best of Both Worlds" and I know I shouldn't let her jump on the bed, but I'm laughing so hard and we're all dancing, and I don't think anyone is going to lose an eye. So she keeps jumping.

Nick doesn't like to join in the shows anymore since he announced he hates "girl songs," so we have to get more creative to spend quality time together. We love to curl up with a good book, usually about whales, sharks, or some endangered species. But sometimes he really wants me to act silly or join him in some crazy boyish stunt, just so I can be part of his world. Last year on spring break, Nick kept begging me to boogie board in the ocean with him. I really hate all the seaweed and shells between my toes, and the thought of getting stung by a jellyfish terrifies me, but there are times when Devoted Mommy just can't say no to him. So I jumped in.

Boogie boarding is quite exhilarating when you get the hang of it. Never mind the sand in my hair, saltwater stuck in my throat, or the fact that I twisted and bruised my shoulder when a giant wave knocked me over and pulled me to the ocean floor. I felt like a teenager again, and I even had an audience. Maybe I could be Superwoman after all. I looked up and a group of people were standing on the shore cheering. Could they be cheering for me? *They probably think I'm one of the cool college girls here for spring break,* I thought to myself. Then I heard a man start chanting, "Go, Mom. Go, Mom." The rest of the crowd started to join in with Nick, who was now yelling at the top of his lungs. Okay, I guess they knew I wasn't a spring breaker after all, but at least I was out there living life large and letting go. When I got to the shore, a guy with a T-shirt that said "I Love Hot Moms" stopped me and said, "Lady, I've got to give it to you. Most moms won't even get up off their beach towels, but not you."

I felt a little embarrassed as I later pulled the sand out of my bathing suit in handfuls. There's a certain age where a woman really shouldn't show that much skin. Aren't mommy capes supposed to be long and modest? I probably looked a little silly out there, but Nick was beaming. It was all for him.

Unconditional Love

As much as I want my kids to think I'm cool, more than anything I want them to know how much I love them. I mean really love them, no matter what. I pray my kids won't get in trouble for skinny-dipping at church camp, but even if they do I'll still love and accept them.

I've never been the best at discipline, and I have lots to learn about tough love. But I also know that each of my children is different, and the only thing they all consistently respond to is unconditional love.

In many ways, Anna is like me—she's motivated by grace. Doug figured this out long before I did, and he always reminds me that if you're overly critical or try to back her into a corner or take away privileges, it completely crushes her spirit and she shuts down, but if you open your arms to praise her good behavior or put a carrot in front of her, she's usually obedient and eager to please. So when Anna won't listen and gets more hysterical than usual, I sit her down, look at her in the eye, and say to her, "Even when you don't listen to Mom, I still love you." It doesn't work every time, but sometimes she gets quiet, she smiles, and then she calms down enough to make a "good choice." There are still consequences to her actions. But she knows I'm going to love and accept her, regardless.

Anna has adopted this approach with the rest of the family. She frequently tells me, "I still love you, Mom, when you yell at me." And she's always telling Abby that we love her, even when she's "bad."

Abby enjoys life to the fullest and pulls more deviant stunts than the other two put together. But the one thing I'm encouraged by is her repentant spirit. Abby is by far the best at saying sorry. Getting

Nick and Anna to say sorry is like pulling teeth; not so with Abby. She'll accept full responsibility, even when it's not her fault. I can't quite figure it out, except that she always wants to restore the relationship. She's genuinely sad when someone else is offended. So even though she's the wildest two-year-old I've ever met, the rest of us have a lot to learn from her.

I hope my kids learn to have unconditional love toward each other, something rare in siblings. When I was in grade school, Artist Sister—who I thought walked on water since she was a cool teenager with long hair and cute boyfriends—looked me in the eye and told me something I'll never forget. She said, "Susie, even if you screw up in life and become addicted to drugs, I'll still think you're great." It stuck with me forever.

Artist Sister really has this unconditional love thing figured out, so I've stolen a few of her lines with my own kids. I like to tell Nick, "If all the first-grade boys in the whole world were standing in a line, and I could only pick one, do you know which one I would pick?" His eyes get wide and he gives me a big grin as I finish. "I would pick *you* every time."

Then I tell Anna and Abby, "I love you and I'm glad you're my daughters. Before you were born, God looked all over the world to decide which family to put you in. He said, 'What family will treat them like princesses, love them the most, and teach them about God?' And after looking long and hard, He decided to give you to me and Dad."

I made that one up myself.

Sometimes I think that if I pray hard enough, keep teaching Sunday school, make sure we have fun in the process, and practice unconditional love, my kids will naturally turn out in the end and follow God. Maybe there's a formula after all.

Then I am reminded that God is in control.

Nonjudging Jane told me there was someone she wanted me to meet. She was mentoring Nicole, a premed student who was raising money for a mission trip. Nicole knew few Christians because she grew up in a non-Christian home. I was intrigued.

I met with Nicole and decided to support her mission trip. She told me about her own conversion to Christianity, and I was completely baffled. Nicole's parents did absolutely nothing to encourage her faith. Her father, a university professor and self-proclaimed atheist, considered Nicole's conversion to Christianity a deep and personal failure of his own. Her mother, while not as openly hostile to Christianity, was disenchanted by the traditional church and would just as well keep her children away from organized religion. Yet somehow Nicole could not resist the calling of Jesus. Against everything her parents had taught her, she embraced a relationship with God with zeal and purpose. In fact, she has more passion about her faith than most Christians I know who are raised in loving, "Christian" homes.

Like Nicole, each of us comes to faith as an individual, not based on life circumstances or genetics. On the other hand, if I smother my children with Christianity, are they going to be rebellious? I've seen too many children raised in traditional Christian homes simply run the other way.

As a parent, it is reassuring to know that God is ultimately in control of bringing my children to faith. But it's also terrifying. It means *I'm* not in control. In other words, once Devoted Mommy teaches Sunday school, reads bedtime stories, acts cool with her kids, and practices unconditional love, she can let go and leave the rest to God. It sounds a little too good to be true. Most of the time, we think that we need to put our kids in the perfect environment—the best schools, the best church, the most stimulating activities, cutting-edge educational experiences, and peer groups who will model good choices. And we actually feel guilty if one of the pieces of the puzzle isn't completely perfect. Working mothers especially feel that we need to overcompensate, so we probably overdo it to reinforce a "positive" environment for our kids. But despite our efforts to control everything we can, at the end of the day we really just need to float.

Floating

Devoted Mommy is jumping into the river with both feet. In fact, I think my own mother approached both motherhood and faith more like a river than a road. Roads are hard, straight, and require a set of wheels or a pair of legs. Most of us get tired of walking and want someone to carry us or at least give us a ride. But a river is different—a river allows you to float. It doesn't mean that you're not prepared for what's ahead or that you don't shape your children's environment, encourage their faith, and help them make good choices. It just means that you can float with the current and allow the Spirit to carry you on the journey, knowing that it's okay to let go.

In *Surrender to Love,* David Benner's description of the river is welcome news for working mothers like me who just need to know that God will never let go, even though we have to.

Surrender to God flows out of the experience of love that will never let me go. It is the response of the heart that knows that since God is for me, nothing can come between me and the perfect love that surrounds me and will support me regardless of my effort, my response or even my attention.

Considering how easy and natural floating is, I am amazed how much energy I expend treading water. The lie I seem to believe is that my efforts are keeping me afloat, perhaps even keep me moving through the water. The reality is that all they do is tire me out, hold me in the same place and deprive me of the joyous discovery that I am supported.

***

Then, in exhaustion, I momentarily surrender. I relax. I allow my full weight to be supported by the Spirit. And not only do I float, I flow with the current. I hadn't even been aware that there was a current. My thrashing about in the water made me oblivious to its presence and force. Now I begin to know what I was fighting.

To fail to go with the flow is to try to push the river. But the river—God's Spirit—doesn't need any help.[2]

Trusting Tracy says that approaching faith like a river has changed her life. So I asked her, "How does this concept of the river work in real life?" Sure, in simple terms it sounds good, but does it really work?

So I gave Tracy a hypothetical. "What do you do if you're running late? After all, it's hard to float when you're in a hurry."

Tracy's answer? "You never rush. Instead you're just going to be late. Humble yourself and apologize." She went on to explain that, when you start to flow with the river, it's difficult to set boundaries and you find yourself baking cookies at midnight for someone you just ran into who needs encouragement because you're just responding to the moment instead of staying in control. Plans tend to change. According to Tracy, the only downside to this way of life is that sometimes she gets less sleep. But approaching life like a river helps her to live in dependence on the Holy Spirit, especially when she feels as if she's going to sink.

It sounded both exhilarating and exhausting. So I gave Tracy another hypothetical. "What if you are having twenty people over for dinner and you forget to prepare?"

She replied, "You decide to just go with the flow."

"Everyone arrives at your house at 6:00 p.m. with no food. What next?"

According to Tracy, again, you humble yourself and apologize. Then, you problem solve. You discover that half of your dinner guests want junk food, and half want healthy food. So you order out both. How else would you have known to buy *both* junk food and healthy food in the first place? So the river is a win-win for everyone, including your guests. Thank God you didn't have a plan.

Tracy's answer makes me laugh hard. I can just picture a bunch of hungry friends arriving at my home for dinner with no food in the house and Doug telling me that again I've bitten off more than I can chew. I still love Trusting Tracy's perspective on life, and I know that hanging out with her helps Devoted Mommy be a better mother. And I really can't wait to meet Jaina.

FIFTEEN

Chasing Superwoman

For it is by grace you have been saved, through faith—and this not from yourselves, it is the gift of God—not by works, so that no one can boast. For we are God's workmanship, created in Christ Jesus to do good works, which God prepared in advance for us to do.

Ephesians 2:8–10

When I was a little girl, I loved superheroes. My favorite cartoon was *Superman and the Hall of Justice.* My favorite character? Wonder Woman.

I always wanted to be Wonder Woman. From my perspective, she seemed to have her act together. She was smart, beautiful, powerful, and always got her way. What more could a woman want?

Now that I am a full-time lawyer, full-time mom, and part-time writer, I could use some of that superhero strength, not to mention the gold wristbands and magic lasso. The gold wristbands would help me fight off Jerk Lawyer and MECHs, and I also need that magic lasso with the truth serum—it would come in handy with the kids, not to mention in the courtroom.

Little girls today are told they too can be superheroes. Anna and Abby like to sing at the top of their lungs, "Who said, who said, I can't be Superman. I say, I say, that I know I can."[1] I don't have the heart to tell them just yet that Superman isn't everything he's cracked up to be. Unfortunately, there's no training manual when you're pretending to be a superhero. At least Lady Lawyer got to go to law school and clerk with the firm. There aren't any Superwoman schools and no paid internships. It's all trial and error.

Superwoman Hits a Brick Wall

Sometimes, I forget I'm not really Superwoman, and I try to attempt the impossible. We all have those experiences when we know we have gotten in over our heads. Working mothers tend to be gluttons for punishment, even though we know deep down that we really can't do it all. So there are certain experiences that even I would never subject myself to a second time. On the top of the list? Flying to Vegas with a five-week old, a two-year-old, and a five-year-old. Alone, of course.

Why would I ever put myself through the utter insanity? It's easy. In addition to the delusion that I can really do it all, I did it for Encouraging Amy. There are only a couple people in this world I would do just about anything for, and she's one of them.

Amy had been begging me to come and visit since she and Jon moved to Vegas several years ago. But between the kids and work, when could I ever find the time? Then, during my maternity leave with Abby I thought, *This may be the only time I can get away for the next decade.* So I bought the tickets and didn't look back.

Doug thought I was crazy. With Anna in the terrible twos and Abby only five weeks old, how would I ever handle all the kids on the plane myself? I invited Doug to come with me, but for some reason he didn't think it sounded like much fun to make the trip with a newborn and two toddlers. In fact, he told me he thought it was a complete waste of time and money, and that I should wait until the kids were at more suitable ages. After I booked the tickets without him, he went and booked a golf trip with his buddies the same weekend. The nerve! I would show him! I'd have more fun, go out on the town late, win lots of money, and have three perfect children on an airplane.

It all came true, except the part about the airplane.

Getting through security was my first obstacle. I had Abby strapped securely in one of those handy-dandy, front baby-carrier slings, freeing up my hands to push Anna in the stroller and hold Nick's hand, while carrying luggage on my back. Unfortunately, all that changed when security made me disassemble the sling and peel Abby off of my body. Apparently they thought all the baby gear was a clever disguise to smuggle drugs across the country. So when I realized I couldn't carry everyone or everything through security, I must have looked completely helpless, and some guy in a white muscle shirt and gold chains ended up feeling sorry for me. He picked up my luggage as I carried my kids and asked, "Where are you going anyway, lady?"

"Vegas," I said.

He responded, "You're nuts, lady."

At this point, I had already figured that out. But it was a little late to turn back.

The flight was hands down the worst four hours of my life. Abby was fussy and restless, and she just wanted to nurse. I really try not to nurse in public, but I figured the circumstances demanded it, even if the guy next to me was a little uncomfortable. Given the choice, he'd probably choose a nursing mother over a screaming baby any day. Everyone knows a five-week-old nursing baby eats every ninety minutes on a good day. After gate check, security, and boarding, Abby was long overdue. At the same time, Anna would not sit in her seat for takeoff, so I had to bribe her with lots of candy and soda, so much that she had to go potty before they turned the seatbelt sign off. I tried to convince her to go pee pee in her Pull-Up, because big girls are allowed to go in their diapers on airplanes. She didn't buy it. So I broke the rules and made the hike to the bathroom with all four of us. Nick stood outside the bathroom, but I couldn't exactly put Abby down in the aisle, so I tried to squeeze into the bathroom while holding Abby. But airplane bathrooms are about one square foot, and the door wouldn't shut with all three of us inside and kept swinging open, and when I stooped down to help Anna pull down her Pull-Up, the door hit poor Abby right in the head. More screaming. Then Anna freaked out over the blue water and ominous toilet seat. I finally calmed everyone down and decided to let Anna go potty by herself, like a big girl.

We stood outside the door and patiently waited, until Anna opened the door, now completely naked. She was going through that phase where she preferred to take all her clothes off to go potty, and I just remember that I wanted to crawl into a corner and cry, but I had nowhere to go so I had to stay strong and pretend to be Superwoman. But clearly I am not Superwoman, because everyone knows she can control her children on airplanes, and mine were screaming and running around naked. The flight attendant started yelling at me and told me that Anna had to get shoes on immediately or she would get hepatitis B. Never mind that she had no clothes on, this woman was more concerned with her feet.

I really don't remember what happened next, except that I started to pray and just sobbed when I got off that plane. Sometimes I ask myself why I try to do it all, because it really hurts when I fall flat on my face.

Choices

Some days, I just feel like I want to give up. Like one day last winter when Nonjudging Jane called to let me know she would be in town the following day. I dropped everything at the office—never an easy task—and met her for coffee. Coffee turned into lunch. I explained to her that the night before I had been driving home in a snowstorm. My twenty-minute commute took two hours, and I didn't get home until after the kids were in bed. I was exasperated. Devoted Mommy was done trying to be Superwoman and announced to God, "I quit. I can't do this anymore."

Nonjudging Jane listened. She didn't tell me that I had to quit my job, or that I had to reorder my priorities, or that I just had to get up fifteen minutes earlier every morning to pray. And she didn't even tell me that I needed to make a list of all the pros and cons in my life stage and then "pray about it." She just listened.

Then I remembered a story she had told me in college. During my junior year I was raising money for an overseas mission trip. Raising several thousand dollars for a college student is no easy task. Encouraging Amy had come to visit me for the weekend, and we were shopping when I saw a beautiful sweater that caught my eye. I had the money, but I felt like it was wrong for me to buy a sweater that I didn't really need at the same time I was asking my friends and family to fork over money for my mission trip. I agonized over the sweater and decided not to buy it. It was painful.

The next day I met with Nonjudging Jane, and I was still stewing over the sweater. I told her that I was proud of myself. I had conquered materialism, and God was looking down on me and smiling. Right?

Nonjudging Jane said, "Do you really think you made the right decision?" She then told me about two of her missionary friends who were raising money for China. At the same time they were raising money for China, they were also praying that God would provide money for a stereo. This raised a few eyebrows among their supporters and friends. Raising money for China was one thing, but a stereo?

Nonjudging Jane's friends weren't bothered by the criticism. Instead, they said, "God doesn't have to choose between China and a stereo."

At that point a light bulb went on. God didn't have to choose between a mission trip and a new sweater. It was all His money anyway. In fact, He didn't even need me for the mission trip. He would accomplish His purposes with or without me.

Several weeks later I saw Encouraging Amy again. She handed me a shopping bag. Inside was the sweater.

Just when I think I have God figured out, He surprises me. I didn't have to choose between the mission trip and the sweater after all. But once I was willing to give up the sweater, it appeared in my closet.

Now you may think this is just a silly story about a sweater and a stereo, but twenty years later I'm still wrestling with the same issues and asking the same questions. Nonjudging Jane reminded me that Devoted Mommy doesn't have to choose between my family and my job, but that sometimes it just feels that way. God is big enough to handle both. Of course, I couldn't see this myself. I had put God in a box. My box. I had bought into the lie that a godly, spiritual mother doesn't work outside the home. I had bought into the other lie that a successful career woman gets ahead only by sacrificing her family.

Labels

One thing I love about being married to Doug is that he is the one person in the world whom I never try to impress or convince I'm Superwoman. I'm always trying to impress everyone else. I want my family and friends to think I'm a good mom, I want my colleagues to think I'm a good lawyer, I want my clients to think I'm smart, I want my kids to think I'm cool, and I want my neighbors to think I'm normal. Okay, maybe I'd settle for half-normal. Anyway, you get the point. It's a lot of people to impress.

But I never try to impress Doug. It's not even intentional. It's just a gift. I think God knows that we are all people pleasers by nature, so He makes sure we have at least one person in our lives that we don't have to impress. In my case, I'm lucky enough to have that person be my husband.

Here's the other thing about Doug—he hates when people try to impress him. So when Lady Lawyer drags him to cocktail parties and social events, he drags his feet reluctantly, never follows the dress code, and ends up spending half the night talking to the bartender about the baseball playoffs or the newest movie. He really doesn't care what people think about him, and he won't try to impress anyone. He doesn't even try to put on a happy face and fake it. So he ends up telling strangers that they have lousy fashion, or he tells the neighbors that he hates the color of paint on their shutters or that new car they just bought is overpriced and overrated. He just tells it like he sees it. The good news? You always know what you're going to get. I have dozens of names for myself, but only one for him. He's just Doug. He knows who he is, and who he isn't.

Sometimes I really hate labels too. At least once a week, someone accuses me of being Superwoman. The problem is, I don't want to be Superwoman. Superwoman has been thrust upon me. What are my options anyway? It's either suck it up and be Superwoman, or change my lifestyle, move out to the country, quit working, and join the PTA. I know it's not that black and white. Sometimes it just feels that way.

Nonjudging Jane likes to ask people, "Who are you?" It's a trick question, of course, but she asks it to make a point.

Most people respond, "I'm a teacher," or "I'm a mother."

Nonjudging Jane will respond back, "No, that's what you *do*. Who *are* you?"

It's been awhile since I've thought hard about who I am, but most of us have our identity wrapped up in what we do. We're totally performance driven. For working mothers, it's easy for us to wrap our identity up in our careers, but it's just as easy to wrap our identities into being mothers. Not just any mother, but a *good* mother with obedient—even doting—children. That is why most of us who work outside the home are utterly crushed when we see our children suffering because we work. What does that say about our identity as *mothers?*

So while I want to be judged on what I do—not some ridiculous label—I think I might crack if my entire identity rides on my performance. As much as I pretend to be Superwoman, my daily life (let alone my experience on airplanes) confirms that it's just not possible to do it all.

This is where grace comes in. As a child of God, I don't have to earn anything. I am holy, blameless, forgiven, and even redeemed by the blood of Jesus. This doesn't give me a license to screw up; it just gives me the freedom to be the best wife, mother, and lawyer that I can be.

Think of the one thing in life you have always wanted to do. Climb a mountain? Go back to school? Start your own business? Even write a book? What if you knew the end result? Before you ever went back to school, you could see your diploma just sitting there, waiting for you. And your report card is sitting right next to it to prove your success—straight As! Now, think how much confidence you would have to go back to school. You don't have to worry about failure, you just have to focus on learning and doing your best. Or what if you knew your book was going to be on the best-seller list before you even wrote it? Wow, what a motivation to write! It doesn't mean it won't be hard and tedious to write the manuscript. You'll go through lots of revisions and you'll be that much more motivated just because you know it will be a success. In fact, you'll even work harder because you recognize the awesome privilege of having a large readership.

So Jane was right after all; it's not what I do that defines who I am. It's *whose* I am, not who I am. I know how the story ends. It ends in the arms of Jesus. It ends with grace, not guilt. And rather than floundering against the waves, I can hold still and float (even flow) with the current.

I love to read my kids the story of Punchinello.[2] Punchinello is a Wemmick who is always getting bad marks. You see, the Wemmicks are wooden people, all made by the woodworker, Eli, and they go around all day putting stars and dots on one another. The stars signify good performance, while the dots represent bad marks. Punchinello has lots of dots. One day he meets another Wemmick, Lucia, who has no stars or dots. "How can this be?" wonders Punchinello. Then Lucia tells him that it's easy—she goes to see the woodworker, Eli, every day and spends time with him. Lucia doesn't care what the other Wemmicks think—they're just Wemmicks after all. But Punchinello still isn't sure. He is completely terrified to go see Eli.

Yet he just can't live in a world of stars and dots, so he decides to take the plunge to go and visit Eli. Punchinello finally decides, "I don't want anyone's stars or dots." So he goes to visit the woodworker, Eli. Just as he begins to understand his true identity, one of the dots falls off like magic.

Like Punchinello, I can't live up to anyone's expectations, including my own. The good news? I don't have to. The more I spend time with my maker—following the Spirit and floating in the river—the less I worry about what other people think.

Maybe Trusting Tracy was right after all. Floating sounds exhilarating, but sometimes I'm just not sure I can let go. The irony, of course, is that when I let go and rest in God's grace, I finally experience the freedom I've been longing for. As David Benner explains,

> *Floating is a good illustration of this, because you cannot float until you let go. Floating is putting your full weight on the water and trusting that you will be supported. It is letting go of your natural instincts to fight against sinking. Only then do you discover you are supported.*[3]

Have I gotten to the point where I don't care what anyone thinks? Of course not. But I don't sit around worrying about what God thinks about me. I know what He thinks. "My grace is sufficient for you, for my power is made perfect in weakness."[4] And approaching life like a river has given me an overwhelming sense of relief. I don't have to be Superwoman anymore. In fact, I don't even *want* to be Superwoman. From what I can tell, Superwoman doesn't exactly have Jesus on speed dial. And she's running, not floating.

I'm tired of running.

So instead of chasing Superwoman, I'm thanking God for His grace and trusting the Spirit to carry me through the waters of motherhood.

What about you?

My Mother's Sauce

I don't use a recipe when I make my mother's sauce. I've seen her make it so many times (and have made it myself so many times) that I can make it in my sleep. Just in case you want to give it a try, here's my best shot at a formal recipe. (Sorry, I never measure.)

Supplies:

- a 16-quart saucepan (the bigger the better—I've moved up to the 20-quart pan)
- a wooden spoon
- a kitchen full of children (optional)

Ingredients:

- olive oil
- garlic (the more the better)

- peppers and onions (optional)
- four to five 28-ounce cans of tomato sauce
- four to five 28-ounce cans of tomato puree
- one to two 28-ounce cans of crushed tomatoes
- Italian spices (basil, oregano—the fresher the better)
- three to four pounds of ground meat
- Italian-style bread crumbs
- two to three eggs
- parsley
- five to seven links of Italian sausage, both hot and mild (I cut them in small pieces after they cook)

Ten Steps to Perfection:

1. Wash your hands.
2. Make someone else (preferably over the age of eighteen) open all the cans of sauce.
3. Sautee garlic, onions, and peppers in a liberal amount of olive oil. Don't burn the garlic!
4. Dump the cans of sauce, puree, and crushed tomatoes into the saucepan (with the olive oil).
5. Add plenty of water (at least three to four empty cans) so the sauce doesn't burn as it cooks.
6. Make and roll your meatballs (ground meat, parsley, bread crumbs, eggs, and more garlic and Italian spices).
7. Drop the raw meatballs one by one into the saucepan.

8. Drop the raw Italian sausage into the saucepan (if you're on a diet, boil the fat out first).
9. Add Italian spices.
10. Stir occasionally and cook all day on low (the longer the better—at least six hours).

A couple of hints (a.k.a. lessons I learned the hard way):

- Don't burn the sauce—put it on the simmer burner, and if it sticks to the bottom of the pan, add water.
- If the meatballs are too mushy, add more bread crumbs. If the meatballs are too hard, add an egg (or some water).
- The best "job" for kids is making meatballs. Just make sure they wash their hands, and try to keep them away from the stove.
- Making sauce is an art, not a science. If you don't have a specific ingredient, feel free to improvise. Experimentation is always encouraged.
- Don't plan on leftovers. If you're smart, you'll freeze over half the pan for individual dinners before your friends and neighbors smell what you're up to.

Questions? Email me at sdimickele@gmail.com or visit my blog at http://susandimickele.blogspot.com.

Notes

Introduction

1 U.S. Bureau of Labor Statistics, "Women in the Labor Force: A Databook," Report 1002 (2007), www.bls.gov/cps/wlf-databook-2007.pdf.

2 The Barna Group, "Americans Not Concerned About Their Spiritual Condition," August 6, 2007, www.barna.org/barna-update/article/12-faithspirituality/98-americans-not-concerned-about-their-spiritual-condition.

Chapter 1: The Superwoman Within

1 Matthew 5:48 (MSG).

Chapter 2: Superwoman Has a Day Job

1 Colossians 3:23.

2 Ephesians 2:10.

Chapter 3: It Takes Children to Make a Mommy

1 Matthew 10:16.

2 Luke 1:56.

Chapter 4: The Daily Grind

1 1 Samuel 1:27.

2 1 Samuel 3:9.

Chapter 6: Superwoman Goes to Hollywood

1 2 Samuel 6:16–23.

2 Proverbs 22:6.

3 Proverbs 31:30.

Chapter 7: Superwoman Goes to Church

1 Matthew 24:10, 12.

Chapter 8: Adventures in Shopping

1 Luke 12:20.

Chapter 9: Generations of Superwomen

1 Acts 2:42.

Chapter 11: When Will I Get Some Rest, God?

1 Matthew 11:28–30.

2 Luke 9:13.

Chapter 12: Will I Ever Be Content?

1 Hebrews 13:5.

Chapter 14: Devoted Mommy

1 Proverbs 22:6 (KJV).

2 David G. Benner, *Surrender to Love: Discovering the Heart of Christian Spirituality* (Downers Grove, IL: Intervarsity Press, 2003), 67.

Chapter 15: Chasing Superwoman

1 Hannah Montana, "Who Said," *Hannah Montana* © 2006 Walt Disney Records.

2 Max Lucado, *You Are Special* (Wheaton, IL: Crossway Books 1997).

3 Benner, *Surrender to Love*, 61–62.

4 2 Corinthians 12:9.